Dewey and Power

TRANSGRESSIONS: CULTURAL STUDIES AND EDUCATION

Scope

Cultural studies provides an analytical toolbox for both making sense of educational practice and extending the insights of educational professionals into their labors. In this context *Transgressions: Cultural Studies and Education* provides a collection of books in the domain that specify this assertion. Crafted for an audience of teachers, teacher educators, scholars and students of cultural studies and others interested in cultural studies and pedagogy, the series documents both the possibilities of and the controversies surrounding the intersection of cultural studies and education. The editors and the authors of this series do not assume that the interaction of cultural studies and education devalues other types of knowledge and analytical forms. Rather the intersection of these knowledge disciplines offers a rejuvenating, optimistic, and positive perspective on education and educational institutions. Some might describe its contribution as democratic, emancipatory, and transformative. The editors and authors maintain that cultural studies helps free educators from sterile, monolithic analyses that have for too long undermined efforts to think of educational practices by providing other words, new languages, and fresh metaphors. Operating in an interdisciplinary cosmos, Transgressions: Cultural Studies and Education is dedicated to exploring the ways cultural studies enhances the study and practice of education. With this in mind the series focuses in a non-exclusive way on popular culture as well as other dimensions of cultural studies including social theory, social justice and positionality, cultural dimensions of technological innovation, new media and media literacy, new forms of oppression emerging in an electronic hyperreality, and postcolonial global concerns. With these concerns in mind cultural studies scholars often argue that the realm of popular culture is the most powerful educational force in contemporary culture. Indeed, in the twenty-first century this pedagogical dynamic is sweeping through the entire world. Educators, they believe, must understand these emerging realities in order to gain an important voice in the pedagogical conversation.

Without an understanding of cultural pedagogy's (education that takes place outside of formal schooling) role in the shaping of individual identity--youth identity in particular--the role educators play in the lives of their students will continue to fade. Why do so many of our students feel that life is incomprehensible and devoid of meaning? What does it mean, teachers wonder, when young people are unable to describe their moods, their affective affiliation to the society around them. Meanings provided young people by mainstream institutions often do little to help them deal with their affective complexity, their difficulty negotiating the rift between meaning and affect. School knowledge and educational expectations seem as anachronistic as a ditto machine, not that learning ways of rational thought and making sense of the world are unimportant.

But school knowledge and educational expectations often have little to offer students about making sense of the way they feel, the way their affective lives are shaped. In no way do we argue that analysis of the production of youth in an electronic mediated world demands some "touchy-feely" educational superficiality. What is needed in this context is a rigorous analysis of the interrelationship between pedagogy, popular culture, meaning making, and youth subjectivity. In an era marked by youth depression, violence, and suicide such insights become extremely important, even life saving. Pessimism about the future is the common sense of many contemporary youth with its concomitant feeling that no one can make a difference.

If affective production can be shaped to reflect these perspectives, then it can be reshaped to lay the groundwork for optimism, passionate commitment, and transformative educational and political activity. In these ways cultural studies adds a dimension to the work of education unfilled by any other sub-discipline. This is what Transgressions: Cultural Studies and Education seeks to produce—literature on these issues that makes a difference. It seeks to publish studies that help those who work with young people, those individuals involved in the disciplines that study children and youth, and young people themselves improve their lives in these bizarre times.

Volume 1
An Unordinary Death...The Life of a Suicide Bomber
Khalilah Christina Sabra
Paperback ISBN 90-77874-36-4 Hardback ISBN 90-77874-37-2

Volume 2
Lyrical Minded
The Critical Pedagogy of Hip-Hop Artist KRS-ONE
Priya Parmar, City University of New York, USA
Paperback ISBN 90-77874-50-X Hardback ISBN 90-77874-64-X

Volume 3
Pedagogy and Praxis in the Age of Empire
Towards a New Humanism
Peter McLaren & Nathalia Jaramillo
Paperback ISBN 90-77874-84-4 Hardback ISBN 90-77874-85-2

Volume 4
Dewey and Power
Renewing the Democratic Faith
Randall Hewitt, University of Central Florida, USA
Paperback ISBN 90-77874-92-5 Hardback ISBN 90-77874-93-3

Volume 5
Teaching, Learning and Other Miracles
Grace Feuerverger, Ontario Institute for Studies in Education, University of
Toronto, Canada
Paperback ISBN 90-77874- Hardback ISBN 90-77874-

Volume 6
Soaring Beyond Boundaries
Women Breaking Educational Barriers in Traditional Societies
Reitumetse Obakeng Mabokela (ed.), Michigan State University, USA
Paperback ISBN 90-77874-97-6 Hardback ISBN 90-77874-98-4

Dewey and Power
Renewing the Democratic Faith

Randall Hewitt
University of Central Florida

SENSE PUBLISHERS
ROTTERDAM / TAIPEI

A C.I.P. record for this book is available from the Library of Congress.

Paperback ISBN: 90-77874-92-5
Hardback ISBN: 90-77874-93-3

Published by: Sense Publishers,
P.O. Box 21858, 3001 AW
Rotterdam, The Netherlands

Printed on acid-free paper

Cover photo: MML

TABLE OF CONTENTS

ACKNOWLEDGEMENTS

John Dewey once wrote that "it is of grace not of ourselves that we lead civilized lives. There is sound sense in the old pagan notion that gratitude is the root of all virtue. Loyalty to whatever in the established environment makes a life of excellence possible is the root of all progress." Therefore, I would like to express special gratitude to Dr. Robert Sherman, Dr. Rodman Webb, Dr. Shirley Steinberg, and Dr. Joe Kincheloe for giving me plentiful opportunity and encouragement to do philosophical work. In various ways these scholars have shown me that philosophy is not a task done in the abstract according to general problems and principles but an activity that takes its reason in specific human problems and on the basis of particular human interests. Bill Gaudelli and Mike Johnson supplied me with endless, invaluable counsel on philosophical matters, and John Reynaud, whose example has informed this work more than he will ever know, provided proof that there are giants living in the land. I also want to thank the members of the Southeast Philosophy of Education Society for listening and responding to various bits and pieces of this manuscript over the years. Bill and Mary Briant not only supplied me with an endless amount of food, shelter, cars, computers, child-care, emotional and intellectual support but have raised me as their own since I was nineteen years old. They set the standard for generosity. Of course, all of the credit for the completion of this work goes to my wife, Kelley Briant Hewitt. For the past twenty years she not only has helped me fight off many raving demons of anxiety but has constantly reminded me to trust my own secrets and to give them a loud voice. Her courage stands unmatched.

JOHN DEWEY AND THE PROBLEM OF POWER

Events of the twentieth and now twenty-first centuries provide compelling evidence for the claim that reason has served to help human beings dominate and oppress each other in the name of the collective good. For example, there has been massive destruction of human life as a result of three world wars and various other so called "peace-keeping" ventures designed to bring about global democracy. A run-a-muck capitalist economy that has encouraged the advancement of technology for the sake of exorbitant profit but touted as the means to equalize the distribution of material necessities has left otherwise avoidable pestilence and poverty in its wake. And, the spiritual numbing and moral fragmenting of community life can be traced to a creeping bureaucratic apparatus set up to administer the good life. The overall effect has led to what Richard Bernstein has called "the rage against reason" and what Max Weber before him saw as the disenchantment with the world.[1]

Thus, it seems that human reason is impotent as the collective means to an ever expanding good life. The glorious tool of the fledgling social sciences charged with helping people liberate themselves from their particular conflicts at the turn of the twentieth century has left them politically docile and apathetic and economic slaves who measure their social value solely on the basis of material accumulated, instead of the quality of their experience with other human beings. And perhaps what the disenchantment with the world has come to signify is their loss of spiritual connection to others in the world. That is, they have lost faith that, when qualified by the give and take of mutual respect and intelligence, their inextricable connection to others can lead to ever wider points of contact that enrich the significance of their individual quests together. In other words, they have lost trust in one of the most intelligible, philosophically consistent, and ethically appropriate ways of acting in a world shot through with difference, risk, danger, and change inherent in the very moment of birth. They have lost trust in the idea that experience can be improved and thus, in effect, have lost trust in themselves.

In *The American Evasion of Philosophy* Cornel West has pointed out that this amelioristic sense of experience got its most mature social and political statement in the practical philosophy of John Dewey.[2] Alan Ryan, in *John Dewey and The High Tide of American Liberalism*, suggests that there is widespread agreement that Dewey represented "thinking America" at its best. But, Ryan goes on, Dewey's way of doing philosophy and thinking about democracy not only became out of vogue during his lifetime but "almost as soon as he died, he was therefore dismissed from the collective mind."[3] And while the philosophical current of postmodernism has created awaking interest in Dewey's way of philosophizing, it runs against and even damns thinking in terms of a universal ideal, an aspect that is vital and central to Dewey's philosophy. A consistent complaint among Dewey's various critics is that while he develops a concept of power as the ability to act and have effect in the world, he does not develop this concept to acknowledge power also as the ability to deceive, manipulate, and dominate. The upshot of Dewey's alleged insufficient concept of power is that it makes his faith in an amelioristic sense of experience and a democratic ideal untenable.

Alan Ryan's idea that there have been two kinds of readers of Dewey is suggestive in clarifying the claim that Dewey has an inadequate concept of power.[4] On the one hand, there are those who see Dewey as a philosophical materialist attempting to undercut the faith in transcendent absolutes (theological or metaphysical). Consequently, Dewey's philosophy leads human interaction into moral anarchy, since it fails to provide any overarching moral principles by which to resolve conflicting value and truth claims. In *The Conservative Mind*, Russell Kirk accuses Dewey of spiritual insolence and, in effect, of morally contaminating society with an "anything goes" attitude so long as it is pleasurable for the greatest number ideal.

The belligerent expansive and naturalistic tendencies of the era found their philosophical apologist in John Dewey. No philosopher's style is more turgid; but Dewey's postulates, for all that, are simple and quite comprehensive. He commenced with a thoroughgoing naturalism, like Diderot's and Holbach's, denying the whole realm of spiritual values: nothing exists but physical sensation, and life has no aims but physical satisfaction. He proceeded to a utilitarianism which carried Benthamite ideas to their logical culmination, making material production the goal and standard of human endeavor. . . . He advocated a sentimental egalitarian collectivism with a social dead-level its ideal; and he capped this structure with Marxist economics, looking forward to a future devoted to efficient material production for the satisfaction of the masses, a planners' state.

Every radicalism since 1789 found its place in John Dewey's system; and this destructive intellectual compound became prodigiously popular, in short order, among the distraught crowd of the semi-educated and among people of more serious pretensions who found themselves in a withered world that Darwin and Faraday had severed from its roots. Intensely flattering to   the presumptuousness of the modern mind, thoroughly contemptuous of authority, Dewey's works were a mirror of twentieth-century discontent; and the picture of the Utilitarian future toward which Dewey led the rising generation was not immediately repellent to a people who had subjected themselves to the lordship of sensation. Veneration was dead in Dewey's universe; indiscriminate emancipation was cock of the walk. This was the imperialistic craving of America and the twentieth century given a philosophical mask.[5]

Not all of those who see Dewey as a materialist object to the threat that Dewey poses for theological and metaphysical absolutes. What these critics object to is that Dewey gives back with one hand what he takes away with the other. That is, while Dewey works to undermine the philosophic foundations of transcendent absolutes, ironically, he argues for the technological administration of the organic good life entailed in the inevitable march of Darwinian evolution. Lewis Mumford, by no means sympathetic with Dewey's religious or metaphysical critics, lumps Dewey as one of those who misunderstands Darwin's organic evolution to mean mechanical social progression. Simply put, Dewey maintains that there is a predetermined state of affairs toward which human beings, aided by their ability to reason, are evolving. Reason, then, particularly as embodied in technology and employed as a tool in regulating human conduct, naturally helps fine-tune human experience in its development toward this culminating state of affairs. Therefore, Dewey sees human intelligence as having only benevolent social consequences and has no idea that intelligence also can lead to social conflict and power relations over others. This mistaken Darwinism, according to Mumford, fails to account for how reason, particularly as embodied in science, can be used against human beigns instead of liberating them.[6]

Like Mumford, Reinhold Niebuhr suggests that Dewey's Darwinian philosophy is politically naive and morally bankrupt, since it fails to account for how reason can be and has been used to dominate and oppress.[7] Both Mumford and Niebuhr imply that this Darwinian philosophy provides the justification and ideological veneer for all sorts of relations of domination and oppression. This hint at philosophical complicity with those who benefit from relations of domination and oppression (or relations of power over) is an idea that Marxists have seized and made the focus of their attack upon liberal democracy in general and upon Dewey's philosophy in particular.

Although they view his philosophy as deficient, the Marxists fall within the second class of Ryan's readers of Dewey: those who see him attempting to cultivate the possibility of a spiritual unity within experience guided by an amelioristic faith in human intelligence. What they object to is that Dewey attempts to subsume or reduce the irreducible and incompatible plurality in experience into one seamless, homogenous flow of becoming. Most recently in *The Promise of Pragmatism*, John Patrick Diggins, though not a self-claimed Marxist, maintains that, because Dewey puts human experience in terms of a biological organism struggling to adapt to its external conditions, he can conceive of power only in terms of the ability to do or have effect. Therefore, power as dominion over other human beings is not a logical possibility in Dewey's thought.[8] "For Dewey not only refused to give much attention to power and its origins, he also had no idea where to look for it other than as some kind of aberration. When Dewey thought at all about power --not as the ability to act and have effect but as control and domination-- he usually interpreted it as an example of dislocation and maladjustment, the failure of education and intelligence to catch up with economic development and the rise of big business."[9]

3

Though some of Dewey's Marxist critics fault his Darwinian metaphysics as the cause of his alleged inability to conceive of power as domination, others such as Herbert Marcuse, Joseph Flay, Quentin Anderson, and John Ryder suggest that underneath Dewey's idea of cooperative inquiry as the method of democracy is a too simplistic assumption that human interaction necessarily is benevolent. In fact, they see Dewey's optimism resting upon two naive assumptions. First, they claim that Dewey views social interaction as a shared exchange of homogenous interests (value). The social problems, then, that stand in the way of achieving these shared interests stem from outdated and unwarranted ideas and assumptions inherited from the past (cultural lag and maladjustment). Second, they maintain, Dewey believes all that is needed to overcome these social problems is human reason as embodied in scientific inquiry aimed at illuminating those handed down assumptions that stubbornly stand in the way of expanding relations of human cooperation.[10] The upshot of Dewey's naiveness is that he fails to provide adequate means to combat the social relations that exploit the common, public good for the sake of private, partisan benefit. As Joseph Flay suggests, Dewey's inability to conceive of power over others not only leaves illegitimate social relations intact but serves to protect the very interests and problems he wants to break up.

> In the face of this inertia the democratic liberal is faced with a paradox: he must choose either to live with this inertia or to employ non-liberal, undemocratic means to defeat it. In either case, liberalism is seriously curtailed. . . .I suggest that the fault actually lies in Dewey's failure to give a full analysis of power and power structures. This again is a fault he shares with liberals generally. There is always postulated or assumed some sort of essential equilibrium or system of couterprevailing powers which will insure at least sufficient strength to forces of change so that the latter can overcome the inertia. Without these countervailing forces there is in principle nothing by which to explain or remove the cyclical inertia of the status quo; for in place of these forces stands a power structure in hierarchical form dominating the socio-political process.[11]

Put in language proper to the philosophical drift of the past twenty-five years, Dewey's philosophy, as Diggins and the others read it, gives voice to the failed project of modernism and the utopian state that it entails. That is, Dewey's experimentalism rests upon the mistaken assumption that human experience progresses in a linear march toward a predetermined state of affairs. This march is guided by human intelligence, which, in piecemeal fashion, discovers the necessary details for the utopian realization and sets up a rationally planned social order that aligns the always contextually specific and self-interested in human interaction to harmonize with the universal standard. As Dewey's critics point out, this project fails because it does not incorporate the possibilities of deep-seated evil, inevitable human conflict, and the uncontrollable impulse to dominate other human beings – all matters of power.

For their part, the postmodernists have turned their attention to how human beings employ ideas and language in order to structure social practices into relations of social control and to hypnotize others to see these relations as naturally fixed beyond human change. To the extent, however, that the postmodernists recognize the need to supplement their analysis of power with some sort of vision or faith, they have evoked Dewey's vision of a democratic community with some reservation.[12] That is, they recognize that Dewey provides the philosophical tools to undercut metaphyscial and theological dogma and to cultivate a warranted sense that human experience contains within itself all the materials necessary for an on-going realization of greater spiritual unity. If the postmodern obsession with power yields a too pessimistic view of the human condition, then, as Cornel West says, Dewey's overly optimistic view of the human condition leads to overlooking particular human conflicts and power. In other words, using Dewey as the light, one cannot see the trees for the forest.[13] For this reason, Ryan suggests that "Dewey rightly praised the scientific attitude but took for granted a malleability and predictability in institutional arrangements that all experience refutes. It is this that allowed him to stop a little book like *Liberalism and Social Action* just where it ought to have begun, urging us to be intelligent but not acknowledging how readily intelligent people trip each other up."[14] Nel Noddings best characterizes the postmodernist's objections to Dewey in her book *Philosophy of Education*, although she provides no explication of the matter.

> Possibly the greatest objections to Dewey's work . . . is that he gave so little attention to the problems of race, class, and gender and that he put such great emphasis on the power of scientific thought to solve our problems. . . . He did not give us much advice on handling race conflicts, pressure-group politics, growing gaps between rich and poor, and the unhappy possibility that science might aggravate rather than ameliorate our problems. Ardent followers of Dewey argue that solutions –or at least promising directions—for these problems can be found in Dewey's work. But the solutions seem to depend on an almost utopian view of democracy. In an age complicated by power struggles and loss of faith at every level and in almost every arena, Dewey seems to many to be naïve.[15]

In effect, in this rage against both reason and the amelioristic sense of experience, we face a spiritual cloud looming to engulf the twenty-first century without the proper analytic tools and poetic vision to avert its wrath. This looming cloud encourages, for example, the development of what Benjamin Barber calls Jihad and McWorld: militant forces of reactionary fundamentalism, on the one hand, rallying around various tribal absolutes and recruiting more soldiers for god and zealous forces of predatory capitalism, on the other, insisting that commercial consumption is the ultimate expression of democratic tenets.[16] The upshot is that this mood would leave us entangled in webs of power and manipulation without promise of earthly salvation.

As it stands, then, cultivating an amelioristic sense of experience guided by a democratic ideal that necessitates a social and political liberalism as its means seems no longer what William James would call a living and momentous option. It is not living because human beings have lost faith in democracy and practical, cooperative reason as a working hypothesis in experience. It is not momentous, the claim goes, because having faith or not in light of the actualities of the twentieth century makes no significant difference in the eternal wax and wane of human conflict.

Faith, however, is not exactly the same thing as an astute analysis and recognition of reality. Faith amounts to the belief in some future state of affairs, even though doubt in this state of affairs actually coming about is still possible. This is not to say that the particular objective conditions within and because of which human beings desperately struggle with each other cannot and do not lead to hopelessness and coldheartedness in outlook. But as long as there is anything that can be called the human experience, there will exist the possibility of a future, the concrete details of which are not completely determined and here yet. As James puts these matters, "The coil is about us, struggle as we may. The only escape from faith is mental nullity."[17]

What sort of faith, then, must we have that is warranted given the nature of our experience together? Are we to rally around dogmatic, rigid principles that exclude all in experience that does not conform to the fixed vision? Are we to assume that there is no chance of a moral vision big enough to include the plurality and tentative in experience? Are we, then, destined to an "us against them" faith in which the winners take all and the losers rot in anguish, despair, hopelessness? Are we to wallow eternally in a cesspool of power struggles, a zero sum and null game in which all human interaction is reduced to nothing more than social fronts in the Goffman sense, manipulation and impression management with no possibility of distinguishing between genuine and ingenuine human communion? Are we to disintegrate because of an egotist ethic, an "I won't attack you but I won't back you" ethos?

Getting clear about Dewey's idea of power can help us do two things. First, it can set us on our way to figuring out what it takes to renew a qualified faith and trust in ourselves and our falliable but ineluctable capacities for passion and reason. Second, it can help rejuvenate a collective spirit aimed at improving the quality of our experiences together and therefore correct us in the belief that we are destined to a life of isolation and conflict because our interests are different.

With both Dewey and James, it can be said that, like it or not, belief and doubt are the essential living attitudes inspiring human life and involve some sort of conduct one way or another. Perhaps the difference "between a life of which the keynote is resignation and a life of which the keynote is hope," as James puts it and Dewey's work underscores, hinges upon our belief that we have power to see what we are about in the world and to conduct every impulse of our beings along our visions.[18] Although Dewey did not write explicitly about power, his way of practicing philosophy gives every indication that his work contains a fuller concept of power than what some of his critics have supposed. This indication is all that is needed to warrant a thorough look into the philosophical quest that Dewey takes up and passes along.

[1] Richard Bernstein, The New Constellation: The Ethical-Political Horizons of Modernity/Postmodernity (Cambridge, Massachusetts: The MIT Press, 1991): pp. 31-56. See also Max Weber, The Protestant Ethic and The Spirit of Capitalism, translated by Talcott Parsons, introduction by Anthony Giddens (New York: Charles Scribner's Sons, 1905/1976).

[2] Cornel West, The American Evasion of Philosophy: A Genealogy of Pragmatism (Madison, Wisconsin: The University of Wisconsin Press, 1989). Tracing out what he calls the themes of voluntarism, ameliorism, and activism passed along in the American pragmatist tradition, West suggests that "it is with Dewey that American pragmatism achieves intellectual maturity, historical scope, and political engagement" (p. 6). See also pages 69-111.

[3] Alan Ryan, John Dewey and The High Tide of American Liberalism (New York: W. W. Norton & Company, 1995): p. 22.

[4] Pointing up the fact that Dewey saw no necessary dichotomy between science and morality, Ryan states, "He insisted only that the experimental outlook could unify them. Since this leaves it less than crystal clear whether 'science' is or is not the answer to all our problems, Dewey has always had two sorts of readers; one has seen him as trying to unite the religious conviction that the world is a meaningful unity with a secular twentieth-century faith in the scientific analysis of both nature and humanity, while the other has seen him as an aggressive rationalist, someone who expects 'science' to drive out faith, and a contributor to the twentieth-century's obsession with rational social management. Perhaps one ought to say that he has had four sorts of readers, since both sorts divide on the merits of the resulting system" (John Dewey and The High Tide of American Liberalism, pp. 21-22).

[5] Russell Kirk, The Conservative Mind (Chicago: H. Regnery Co., 1953): pp. 418-419.

[6] See Lewis Mumford, The Myth of The Machine: The Pentagon of Power (New York: Harcourt Brace Jovanovich, Inc., 1964/1970): p. 392.

[7] Reinhold Niebuhr, Moral Man and Immoral Society: A Study in Ethics and Politics (New York: Charles Scribner's Sons, 1932/1960): pp. xii-xv, 35.

[8] This is the same criticism of Dewey's thought suggested by C. Wright Mills some years earlier in his posthumously published doctoral dissertation, Sociology and Pragmatism: The Higher Learning in America, edited by Irving Louis Horowitz (New York: Paine-Whitman Publishers, 1964).

[9] John Patrick Diggins, The Promise of Pragmatism: Modernism and The Crisis of Knowledge and Authority (Chicago: The University of Chicago Press, 1994): p. 288. Comparing the thought of Dewey and Henry Adams, Diggins maintains that "for Dewey, however, power is simply potency and efficacy, not an alien entity but the human ability to translate thought into action and desire into deed; and interest, rather than suggesting a violation of ideals, is simply what concerns us and commands our attention. . . . To Dewey power and interests could hardly invoke the specter of commerce and corruption that haunted Adams, nor could science and technology be anything but benevolent" (p. 215). See pages 280-321.

[10] See Herbert Marcuse, "John Dewey's Theory of Valuation," John Dewey: Critical Assessments III, edited by J. E. Tiles (New York: Routledge, 1992): pp. 22-27; Quentin Anderson, "John Dewey's American Democrat," John Dewey: Critical Assessments II, edited by J.E. Tiles (New York: Routledge, 1992): pp. 91-108; and John Ryder, "Community, Struggle, and Democracy: Marxism and Pragmatism," John Dewey: Critical Assessments II, pp. 337-349.

[11] Joseph Flay, "Alienation and the Status Quo," John Dewey: Critical Assessments II, p. 310, pp. 307-319.

[12] Samuel Bowles and Herbert Gintis mark the place of Dewey in the updated marxist and postmodern frameworks when they say, "Dewey's overall framework seems imminently correct. His error lies in characterizing the social system as democratic, whereas, in fact, the hierarchical division of labor in the capitalist enterprise is politically autocratic"(Schooling in Capitalist America: Educational Reform and the Contradicitons of Economic Life; New York: Basic Books, 1976: p. 46).

[13] West, The American Evasion of Philosophy, p. 101.

[14] Ryan, John Dewey and The High Tide of American Liberlism, p. 369.

[15] Nel Noddings, Philosophy of Education (Boulder, Colorado: Westview Press, 1995): p. 38.

[16] Benjamin R. Barber, Jihad VS. McWorld: Terrorism's Challenge to Democracy (New York: Ballantine Books, 1995/2001).

[17] William James, The Will to Believe: And Other Essays in Popular Philosophy (New York: Dover Publications, Inc., 1897/1956): p. 93.

[18] William James, The Varieties of Religious Experience (New York: Penguin Books, 1901-02/1958): p. 433.

CHAPTER TWO

BACKGROUND TO DEWEY'S THOUGHT: REALISM AND IDEALISM

According to his critics, Dewey's portrayal of human experience in terms of a biological organism adapting to its environment logically locked him into a metaphysical stance in which the organism necessarily evolves according to some predetermined plan existing outside of but working through this organism. Implicit in their complaint is the suggestion that Dewey's work rests upon a two-world dualism. That is, they take Dewey to be saying that a transcendent world of infinite meaning directly causes the effects in the world of finite experience, a relation not subject to human modification. And although conflict and struggle are at the heart of finite experience, these are, simply, inherent manifestations of the transcendent world working itself out according to its own predetermined plan. Therefore, the particular conflicts experienced by human beings inevitably become resolved in this predetermined working out. Thus, a concept of power as the human ability to direct conduct toward some self-defined end, not to mention power to manipulate and control other human beings for some selfish gain, is not a logical possibility in Dewey's work.

As Dewey himself acknowledges, he began his professional philosophical career by assuming the Hegelian tradition, a line of thought that entails a two-world metaphysical stance in which the finite experiences of human beings serve as partial realizations of a predetermined Absolute.[1] It also is true that Dewey developed research from physiological psychology, particularly relating to the biological organism adjusting itself to its environment, as the foundation from which he elaborated his epistemological, social, and ethical insights. Both of these influences on Dewey grew out of a broader philosophical legacy from the 16th Century empiricists and rationalists that had a defining impact on the direction of American philosophy from its beginnings, as Bruce Kuklick points out.[2] In essence, the empiricist and rationalist traditions shaped the subsequent philosophical focus on the epistemological problem of knowing the universal laws underlying experience. Their responses to this problem entailed a delineation of the human capacities to know these laws for certain and a development of the social and ethical implications derived from their metaphysical and epistemological ideas. On the one hand, the insights from both these traditions provided the epistemological foundation from which later psycho-physiological inquiry and the ethical principles underlying self-realization which became the chief tenets of the democratic ideal in America developed. On the other hand, these traditions were tainted with a malignant two-world dualism that permeated everything in their heritage. Their common, unquestioned assumption of immutable laws guiding human conduct from the outside introduced the old dualism between mind and matter into their epistemological claims, which, in effect, undercut their attempt at a consistent account of human experience and self-enlightenment. In a sense, these traditions contained all of the philosophical ingredients necessary to formulate a conception of power as it comes from the human ability to change conduct in light of particular circumstances, which, in broad terms, entails the ability to enrich or to diminish the meaning of experience. However, their steadfast metaphysical position locked them into a disembodied conception of power in which the human being was simply a mechanism for the realization of some realm of meaning independent of human experience.

Given these influences on Dewey by way of Hegel, it is possible that Dewey could have developed an idea of the biological organism predetermined to evolve toward some Absolute, fixed end. That is, it is possible that Dewey simply and uncritically carried over this metaphysical, epistemological, and ethical legacy into psycho-physiological concepts. If this is the case, then his critics would have a justifiable claim that Dewey's conceptual equipment kept him from developing an idea of power that includes the ability to have an effect both on and over others. Therefore, in this chapter it is necessary to spell out this legacy in enough detail, particularly in terms of the problems, assumptions, and concepts handed down, in order to get a clearer sense of the philosophical direction that Dewey took up. In turn, these details will provide sufficient insight to follow the critics' claim through Dewey's work in order to see if this claim bears out or not.

THE PHILOSOPHICAL LEGACY OF THE EMPIRICIST AND RATIONALIST TRADITIONS

Perhaps it was by accident that the natural philosophers of the 16th Century unleashed a prophecy of new tendencies that not only challenged Christian authority but worked to domesticate its transcendent truth and reason for the benefit of secular purpose. Already by the end of the 14th Century, the German bishop and philosopher Nicholas of Cusa had questioned the human ability to know the certainty of God. And by the beginning of the 16th Century, Copernicus's notion that the earth orbited the sun had threatened the Ptolemaic system, by which Christian theology had established its doctrines and political practices as the supreme revelations on earth, the fixed point and center of God's universe. The fact that the Inquisition burned Italian astronomer Giordano Bruno at the stake for extending Copernicus's ideas to suggest an infinitely developing universe points out how strong this threat was to the Christian order of things. However, it was Galileo's invention of the telescope and his experiments with rolling small balls down an inclined plane that provided the concrete means needed to demonstrate that the ideas of his scientific predecessors were not mere fantastic ramblings.

Galileo came to notice a consistency in force and movement when balls of a given weight rolled from a specific distance along an inclined plane. He then pointed out that the consistency of this physical movement could be mathematically signified and predicted. What Galileo's demonstration implied was that if earth-bound bodies move in mathematically predictable fashion, then cosmic bodies also might exhibit change in a similar consistent and predictable way. The invention of the telescope brought the workings of the unfathomable sky closer to the certainty of human sense and mathematical understanding. However, Galileo's scientific insights entailed social and political implications of a more important note. They worked empirically to confirm Copernicus's solar system and Bruno's idea of a continuous, infinitely encompassing universe. In turn, these confirmations increasingly jeopardized the certainty of God and his divine order in light of a universe developing according to natural and physical laws discernible to all human beings. Furthermore, Galileo's insights marked the beginnings of a social and political revolution characterized by the celebration of human beings' capacity to sense, understand, and reason for themselves. What they would come to understand were the encompassing physical laws governing their universe. And through their use of reason, they would come to liberate themselves from binding tradition and illegitimate authority. However, several important questions remained.

While the natural philosophers, in effect, equalized the access to both truth and reason, human beings still were subject to all that was erratic, deceptive, and particular in experience. By what means, then, could human beings come to know for certain the constant natural laws underlying change? What role would reason play in liberating the human experience from the restraints of the past? And as individuals liberated themselves from this past in order to see their experience in the universe as one coming to be, toward what exactly would their liberation lead? Two separate lines of thought, empiricism and rationalism, emerged from the 16th Century to answer these underlying epistemological questions.

The empiricists (from Bacon, Hobbes, Locke, Berkeley, and Hume to J. S. Mill and the 19th Century positivists) held to a metaphysical and epistemological realism. To them, the phenomenal world, including its many parts and cause-effect relations, was unified according to the universal laws independent of but regulating all natural motion and given to human experience through the senses. Human sensation, emotion, and action –all registers of motion—were subject to the same universal laws. Human sense, then, was the concrete point at which human beings had immediate perception of external facts and their relations. All knowledge that was definite and certain could be gathered only through direct sensory impressions of the immediate phenomena. Abstract representations of the world such as ideas and thoughts that were not conduced by direct sense were nonexistent. For example, an entity such as God lacked direct sensory evidence and therefore was impossible. Thus the human mind simply served as an idle filtering device for incoming sensations that, in turn, tripped the faculty of reason into operation. The role of reason, then, was to sort through these particular sensory perceptions, abstracting relations of similarity between facts and testing them for consistency with known laws as mathematically signified. Those relations corresponding to mathematical laws were identified as the correct and natural relations, and those that could not be empirically and mathematically represented were discarded as the false and deceptive relations of custom and tradition. Therefore, human action, as a direct effect of sensory stimulation, could be brought under mathematical prediction and control by regulating the external organization of society according to known universal laws. The metaphysical implications of Galileo's findings, however, were broad enough for two modes of thought to emerge. If these findings suggested to the empiricists an epistemological stance founded upon human sense, it also pointed out to the rationalists that human sense was easily deceived and that appearances, even when viewed through the strength of the telescope, could not be trusted. It was out of this mood of doubt that Rene Descartes and those later known as the rationalists (including, Spinoza, Leibnitz, Kant, and Hegel) came to claim the superiority of human thought.

To Descartes, Galileo's discoveries had deflated the long established Christian workings of the absolute God whereby human beings had made sense of and had taken for granted their assured deliverance from their plight on earth. Furthermore, these discoveries made plain that the human senses had been deceived by appearance. The general certainties that could be derived from sensual experience still were subject to the upsetting uncertainties of future experience. Since human beings were doomed to sensual bodies enveloped within the subtle and therefore tricky folds of appearance, human sense could not be the sound epistemological source for universal knowledge. According to Descartes, all that was certain was the thought of doubt about human sense. The fact that human beings were conscious of their doubt led Descartes to assert that human thought itself, even in doubt, was certain. Thus, the source of all knowledge as certain was the human mind; the objects of this knowledge were the constant laws guiding the process of thought itself.

The rationalists agreed with the empiricists that there was an ideal world of reality independent of human experience. However, this ideal order holding together the world's diverse forms and relations was known in human experience only through the mind and not through the easily deceived senses. In this sense, then, the rationalists held to an epistemological nominalism in which the human mind served as a conduit through which the power of universal reason surged to illuminate the details of the world with order and meaning. According to the rationalists, certainty of knowledge in thought required deducing order from the complete set of universal laws innate to the human mind. But while in the immediacy of their practical endeavors, human beings called up these laws in dumb, piecemeal fashion through intuition. Consistency and certainty in their conduct were haphazard in effect. The rationalists maintained that certainty and consistency in thought and conduct could be affected by turning one's conscious attention onto one's immediate intuitions. This reflection of thought back onto intuition allowed individuals to focus on and locate the abstract cause-effect relations innate to their minds and given in the form of simple ideas. Each idea had to be analyzed for its inherent connection to other ideas. These connections, when traced out systematically, would provide a more insightful, certain, and consistent direction for human life.

Since the mind's ideas could be represented concretely, the pure abstractness of the universal laws could be approximated best by mathematical symbols, collected and applied over time. By applying the already known natural laws as the cause of conduct, human beings could determine the logical course of such conduct, like deducing the unknown angle of a triangle by the subtraction of the sum quantity of the known angles from the constant quantity of the whole. Thus, the particular consequences of human conduct, and therefore collective experience, could be predicted and controlled through mathematical deduction. But, although both traditions held steadfast to the idea of immutable laws guiding human conduct, each tradition provided its own epistemological starting point that, as it turned out, was predicated upon the old dualism between mind and matter. As a result of this dualism, each tradition, when taken separately, could provide only an unbalanced account of self-enlightenment.

According to the strict logic of their epistemological stance, the empiricists could not explain how it was that human beings come to think of an ordered world without immediate sensory impression but verified by sense in some future experience. For example, how could human beings think the idea that tomorrow will be similar to today? On the basis of the empiricist account, human beings could experience only the phenomenal world, that is, only what was actual and as is. Because the empiricist idea of the human mind amounted to a passive sieve that filtered a world of matter, there was no way to the non-phenomenal world of ideas entailing some future state of affairs in which spatially and temporally disjointed impressions of matter become an integrated world for resolute conduct. Thus, the empiricists left the power of reason impotent as a means by which human beings envision and modify the course of their conduct with reference to the world of matter. The upshot of the empiricist account, therefore, was a world of matter standing over and against the powerlessness of the human mind.

The rationalists, on the other hand, had no way of explaining how abstract ideas caused a world of various, and sometimes contradictory, detail. For example, how could the idea of a God as the benevolent creator of all things lead to the conditions of human poverty and misery? Holding to an ideal given a priori to the mind, the rationalists could explain neither causation of an external world by the mind nor the occurrence of facts that were discordant or contradictory to the supposedly already complete ideal. Thus, the rationalists set the power of the mind over and against the concrete temporal demands of human necessity and conflict, thereby undercutting the human capacity to attend to and change that which matters to a thriving human experience. Given the dualism between mind and matter to correct, two lines of thought developed in an attempt to fasten the epistemological claims of the empiricists and rationalists into a consistent and coherent account of human experience. These two lines were Scottish Realism and the philosophy of Kant and Hegel, both lines of which had a significant impact on American philosophy in the 18th and 19th Centuries.

THE 18TH AND 19TH CENTURY LEGACY OF THE BRITISH AND RATIONALIST TRADITIONS

Scottish Realism

Emerging from the empiricist tradition, the Scotsmen Thomas Reid (1710-1796) and his disciple Sir William Hamilton (1788-1844) inherited the problem of cultivating a spiritual ideal out of the empiricist overemphasis on sensory experience. Reid wanted to retain sensory impressions as an epistemological necessity in order to have knowledge about experience, but wanted to avoid the barren, mindless flux that resulted from the empiricists' development of it. More specifically, Reid wanted to circumvent the skeptical conclusion reached by David Hume, that the mind could know only the discrete sensory impressions of an external world and had no evidence for knowing any real relations, particularly causal relations, obtaining between a material self and material objects. To Reid, this skepticism, though understandable given the unquestioned assumptions it entailed, was nothing more than outright lunacy.[3] He not only worked out the deficiencies in the empiricist and rationalist traditions but reminded subsequent philosophers of the more ancient and authoritative principles taken for granted by all human beings, the principles of common sense.

According to Reid, there were only a few principles necessary to avoid the dualism between mind and matter: one, to trust the existence of external objects as real on the basis of testimony from the senses, and, two, to define and judge the relations between qualities of external objects gathered by the senses on the basis of testimony from consciousness.[4] This is to say that this dualism is not a consideration for the everyday person intent on his or her work. The carpenter, for example, does not stop nailing boards together to question the existence of the sun bearing down upon his neck, nor of the hammer in one hand or the board and nail in the other. He does not have to wait until each time he smashes his thumb with the hammer to get the idea of pain or to remind himself that he should be careful to watch the nail head. In other words, he does not need an elaborate philosophical argument to convince himself that a material world of various qualities exists about which he feels and thinks.

As Reid suggested, the trust that human beings have about a substantial world corresponding to their sense of one is a taken for granted characteristic of human existence. This world contains an infinite variety of objects and their relations, some of which are continuous with others, and some not. Human beings know this world of matter to exist because it produces a change or an impression upon their sensory organs, through which they come to perceive this change and to understand its prevailing effects –because they have felt them before—as so much pressure, attraction, repulsion, or vibration. Somehow, according to Reid, these impressions leave a residue of effects or qualities on the nerves and the brain that human beings have the unaccountable capacity to recall. This unaccountable capacity is what Reid called the original faculty of memory, out of which develops all other mental functions, such as simple apprehension, analysis, conception, judgment, and imagination.[5]

To have an idea of a thing, or to conceive of a thing, is to have the ability to recall its previously felt effects, including the bodily response it produced. Memory, then, provides the basis from which individuals analyze or sort out the stream of incoming impressions produced by an external world into their qualitative similarities and differences. Furthermore, memory provides the conceptual basis whereby individuals call an idea of a thing to consciousness without any direct impression of the thing on their senses. This ability to recall the memory of the previously felt effect of a thing is to refer to or to imagine the past effect as the possible or future effect of the thing given similar circumstances. According to Reid, the versatile faculty of memory coupled with the inexplicable power to give physical direction to both body and thought allow human beings to regulate their conduct with ends in view such that they may come to recognize and avoid the detrimental consequences of their actions and to imagine and produce the more beneficial ones. Individuals, then, come to conceive of that which is good for human experience in general as they feel and reason their way through a world of particulars.[6]

According to Reid's epistemological stance, the human experience –and knowledge of it—is encased within a psycho-physiological circuit of matter, sensation, thought, and action. Paradoxically, however, this circuit is not a closed loop that leaves the human being simply as a mechanical extension of radioactive matter or an automaton controlled by unconditioned innate ideas. Due to the plurality of matter, to the human ability to sense, remember, conceptualize, and anticipate the prevailing qualities of matter, and to the human ability to regulate body and thought in order to modify surroundings, this circuit remains open to a current of energy that changes in qualitative magnitude according to the particular reaction between individuals and their world. Therefore, on the basis of Reid's epistemological account, human beings can come to know and understand experience with greater insight only as they continue experiencing. Hence, Reid's answer to Hume's skepticism about causality does not rely on some super-experiential realm; causality comes to be those experienced effects that produce further effects in some direction about which human beings can sense and think. Knowledge that transcends the human capacity to experience it is not possible for human beings. Thus, Reid's epistemological account preserves a spiritual ideal in two senses. On the one hand, human beings have the capacities to conceive of that which is good and perfect for further human experience and to conduct themselves toward this end. In this sense, Reid's epistemological account implies a concept of power that entails the human ability to conceive and realize an ideal as it emerges out of and is embodied in particular human activities. This ability may be called the power of self-realization. On the other hand, that human beings have these capacities constitutes the fundamental data of common sense, but to account for how these capacities come about in the first place, to account for the bare phenomena of existence itself, is beyond the human ability to know for certain and has to be relegated to the unknown. This leaves open the possibility of a supreme creator or a god that can be taken only on faith without any direct experiential warrant.[7] It is this possibility of the unknown that Sir William Hamilton retrieved out of Reid's work and refreshened.

In the "Editor's Supplementary Dissertations" to Reid's works, Hamilton maintains that Reid failed to make an adequate distinction between presentative or intuitive knowledge and representative or mediate knowledge.[8] That is, on the basis of Reid's development of human perception, all that can be known are the external effects of objects as they appear to the individual who feels and thinks his way through the world in the particular. This is knowledge mediated by the human capacities of sense, perception, and thought. Therefore, according to Hamilton, such knowledge as this cannot be certain and universal but must remain relative to human beings and subject to change according to their spatio-temporal conditions. Hamilton suggested that Reid's development of perception left room for ambiguity and confusion about noumena, that is, about objects stripped of their apparent qualities such that all that remain are the bare things in themselves, like peach seeds stripped of their flesh. To Hamilton, knowledge about the noumenal realm was presentational knowledge, and to make mediate knowledge more certain and universal, Hamilton developed Reid's idea of perception to include this noumenal realm.

In order to anchor Reid's idea of perception in the supposedly more certain noumenal realm, Hamilton reinserted into Reid's epistemology the old distinction between primary and secondary qualities of phenomena. According to Hamilton, the apparent effects of external objects that were sensed, perceived, and conceptualized by the human being were the mediated effects or secondary qualities of the things in themselves (the primary effects). That is, objects have primary qualities such as spatial extension, texture, and vibration that are not perceived directly by human beings but become known only through intuition and inference from the mediated or apparent effects (the secondary qualities) on the human nervous system. The noumenal world of primary qualities, then, cannot be known directly but may be intuited as the cause of what human beings do know. This mediated knowledge of the noumenal realm is what Hamilton called the relativity of knowledge. Furthermore, because human beings must subject all phenomena to their capacities of sense and thought, they never can get directly at the noumenal realm as it exists unconditioned. This is what Hamilton called the philosophy of the conditioned.[9]

As Herbert Schneider has pointed out, by the 1820s American philosophers in colleges and universities, primarily religious fortresses until the early 1900s, were using the possibility of the unknown in Reid's work to secure their religious doctrines from the challenges posed by scientific developments.[10] Reid's work gave these philosophers enough speculative room to assert a fixed and complete universe by design and the epistemological means to suggest that it is human beings who are continuously coming to know this design by piecing together its detail. By the 1830s, however, scientists in the fields of geology, chemistry, botany, zoology, and biology had amassed further evidence not only to support the old claim that the natural world, including human beings, is dynamic and evolving, but to suggest that this change is an organic by-product of species-environment interaction. Thus, American philosophers seized upon Hamilton's work as a justification whereby they could avoid the epistemological dualisms of mind and matter, make room for empirical inquiry into everyday phenomena, and yet maintain the existence of the unknown in some sort of causal relation with phenomena accessible to human intuition but exceeding human reason. Therefore, although Reid's work entailed an idea of power as self-determination, Hamilton's work reasserted an idea of power as the control over this self-determination by some nebulous force outside of human experience not subject to human change. By courting the possibility of the unknown as the ground of human perception, these philosophers and theologians had speculative leeway to argue for God's existence and for their own special religious doctrines. More importantly, the combination of Reid's and Hamilton's work allowed them to co-opt science as a tool in the pursuit of a higher ideal and, at least for a while, to ward off the damaging effects of religious skepticism and philosophical materialism.[11]

The Rationalism of Kant and Hegel

If the Scots were concerned with teasing out a spiritual ideal from the empiricist tradition, Kant was just as concerned with providing an empirical ground for the spiritual ideal developed within the rationalist tradition. Kant wanted to account for how human beings connect the bits and pieces of external material impressed upon their senses into a continuous flow such that they come to have a unified experience. More importantly, he wanted to account for how human beings have the capacities to perceive and to conceptualize these bits and pieces before they sense them. To Kant, the ability to perceive and conceptualize had to be prior to any particular sensation in general, otherwise human beings could not give unity to anything that they sensed.[12] He maintained, however, that the rationalists' epistemological trouble --that of explaining how innate ideas cause a material world-- could be cleared up by showing that the a posteriori judgments emphasized by the empiricist tradition are necessary to evoke and guide the a priori judgments stressed by rationalist thought. In other words, sensory experience initiates the mind's innate ideas, and thus the body, into action. What allows human beings to understand the meaning of external phenomena, to give meaningful unity to the infinite plurality of impressions, are just so many ideas and conceptions derived from what amounts to a universal table of conceptual categories given a priori to the mind through the ubiquitous current of universal reason. Without the categories, the unity given to the sensory impressions, and therefore experience, would not be possible; without external phenomena to stimulate an empirical consciousness to use reason, these categories would have no material to synthesize and would remain abstract forms.

Because the empirical consciousness (that is, a concrete person who thinks) is always in a transient spatio-temporal relation with external matter, this consciousness never can know matter in its pure, unchanging state ("the thing in itself") but can categorize and hence understand only the apparent qualities of

17

matter within the limits of a particular space and time. Therefore, according to Kant, this empirical consciousness, whose thought is always conditioned by the specific spatio-temporal relations that it enters into, can define and understand itself only on the basis of its finite relations. That is, a person can understand himself only as a concrete person who, for example, presently teaches at the University of Florida, or as a person who cowed yesterday in the face of four-foot surf but determined to be more courageous the next time the ocean swells. However, as Kant suggested, the various empirical identities of a person presuppose a higher condition in which these various identities become synthesized by one consciousness that thinks about and understands them all: the transcendental apperception, or what amounts to a conscious self (self-consciousness).[13]

Since phenomena and the empirical self are defined and integrated by the universal categories working through the higher self-consciousness, the highest form of human knowledge is self-knowledge. But although the universal categories are innate to the human mind, to know them as the unifying basis for self-consciousness can be done only by understanding this conscious self in its concrete manifestations. Thus, human knowledge of phenomena emerges through the on-going synthesis between the mind's innate ideas and sensory impressions of external phenomena. Likewise, self-knowledge –and therefore knowledge of the categories—emerges through the on-going awareness of one's various particular experiences moving as a unified whole in some distinct direction with some definable quality. The pursuit of self-knowledge, according to Kant, should focus on clarifying the universal categories as they work through the human body. In turn, this clarification or reflection upon the categories should provide a more clear and stable basis (because they are universal and therefore not subject to time and space) whereby individuals can resolve particular conflicts in their experience that are caused by misapprehension or ignorance. Simply put, then, self-knowledge emerges from and enlightens experience. Sensual experience provides the medium through which the mind can come to recognize higher and higher generalizations that, in turn, become the a priori ideas for guiding future experience.

If, however, sense of a finite world is necessary for thought and if thought merges back into sense, how is it possible for human beings to recognize the certainty of the universal categories apart from their finite manifestations? Furthermore, if the universal categories are innate to all human beings, how is it possible that human beings existing within the same context disagree over meaning about their world? Kant provided no epistemological means by which human beings could break free of their finite conditions in order to recognize the certainty of the universal. The upshot was a metaphysical dualism between a supposedly universal table of meaning and a spatio-temporally conditioned mind. Kant's insistence on this universal table of meaning as the immutable guide determining all human conduct undercut the human ability to account for the particular sources of conflict in experience and to modify these sources with a more enriched experience in view. Kant's work, however, was not completely barren of suggestion that would help overcome this dualism. To Kant's successor, G. W. F.

Hegel, Kant's notion that knowledge proceeds synthetically provided at least a start toward resolving the dualism.

Like Kant, Hegel maintained that there is a metaphysical state of pure, unconditioned meaning, what he called the Absolute, that is, a unified whole in which the essence of all phenomena and their relations, including their agreements and contradictions, become harmoniously integrated. Also like Kant, Hegel pointed out that the all encompassing force of reason animates human bodies with ideas derived from the Absolute that, in turn, are stimulated into use through the nervous system. [14] But because the human body is always contextually dependent, human beings have no way to step outside of their particular spatial and temporal relations in order to see and know the complete whole of all relations. What they can perceive, understand, and know are the bits and pieces of this Absolute as they are manifested in the particular felt qualities of things in their context. Simply put, an individual's knowledge of the Absolute is always partial to the quality and quantity of his or her particular experiences in the world.

In a sense, Hegel did not differ from Kant in his understanding of the psycho-physiological means by which human beings come to sense and to know the world; his epistemological account was different from Kant's insofar as he underscored conflict and change as metaphysical and, therefore, epistemological necessities. On the one hand, Kant had suggested that human knowledge of the universal categories always emerges from sensory experience. Thus, knowledge builds from part to part in order to complete the whole. On the other hand, Kant maintained that the universal categories were given to the human mind as a completed whole, or, to put it differently, the whole was already in the part. The implication, then, is that regardless of circumstance, individuals should come to recognize the same meaning and value in the world without discrepancy. Hegel dropped the idea that the whole is completely manifested in the part and hung on to the notion that knowledge of the universal only can be emergent in parts, which gave him room to account for conflict and change in human affairs.

According to Hegel, what allows human beings to distinguish phenomena in terms of their similarities and differences is the fact that every idea or concept of a thing presupposes its opposite or alternative in the great web of absolute relations. In other words, the human experience is one of necessary differences. If differences were not experienced, then there would be no need to distinguish one thing from the next and therefore no need for concepts and ideas. However, according to Hegel, a thing experienced can have meaning only because its concept implies a relation to other things that are different.[15] That is, the concept "red" can have meaning only because it implies some other concept of color that is different and that warrants a distinction to be made, such as the difference between "red" and "blue," for example. Thus, sadness implies its difference as happiness, hard implies soft, conflict implies agreement, sin implies virtue, lunacy implies sanity, and vice versa to infinity.

Since human beings come to a conceptual understanding of their experiences as they are conditioned by particular circumstances, their conditioned knowledge is always a partial knowledge. In order to have a fuller knowledge, individuals must experience or think the opposite of their immediate experience. For example, a person who sees love as bitter can gain a more complete understanding of love only as he comes to experience love as sweet, yielding a synthesis of bitter-sweet. A person who has been conditioned to be a mule of labor can arrive at a more enlightened understanding of himself by experiencing what it is like to take the reins of the mule. Because each individual's experience is a partial manifestation of the Absolute, and always presupposes its opposite, conflict among parts is inevitable and necessary in order to reach higher generalizations not only about experience but, more importantly, about the Absolute. Therefore, change in human experience comes about through the conflict and resolution (synthesis) of partial understandings about this experience.

On the one hand, Hegel underscores the human abilities to sense, think, and act not only as the motors of change but as the powers of self-determination that develop organically in response to the particular conflicts arising from within experience. On the other hand, Hegel's idea of a predetermined Absolute realizing itself by working out its inherent contradictions through human experience issues forth the very same dualism that Hegel wanted to correct in Kant's work in the first place. That is, on the basis of Hegel's account, finite human beings have no other epistemological means to know this predetermined plan as the Absolute except as they act in reference to the particular problems that they face. They may call their concrete actions determined by the Absolute in hindsight, but they have no way of knowing beforehand what detailed conduct this Absolute demands of them. Thus, similar to Kant before him, Hegel's metaphysical claim is superfluous in its account of a realm independent of human experience determining this experience from the outside. Furthermore, this metaphysical claim overshadows the powers of self-determination that Hegel wanted to point up and, in effect, leaves these powers as simply mechanisms of some vacuous, transcendent realm outside of human control.

It is understandable, however, as Herbert Schneider has noted, that America in the 1860s and 1870s provided a fertile ground for Hegel's ideas to take root and grow.[16] Hegel's idea of an Absolute reached through the inevitable conflict and resolution of ideas terminating in time provided a fitting vision for a country ravaged first by civil war and then by an ensuing economic opportunism. That this Absolute could be reached from within experience underscored an organic unity between a higher cause and the human abilities of reason and collective action. Simply put, Hegel's work restated and celebrated in philosophic terms a long since experienced faith by Americans that human reason will wring out everyday conflict from the relentless human effort to bring about a more unified social experience.

THE AMERICAN PHILOSOPHICAL CONTEXT

According to Bruce Kuklick, in *The Rise of American Philosophy*, the particular conceptual framework of the empiricist-rationalist traditions, including the enduring questions of ultimate reality and of how this reality was to be known, permeated the philosophical climate of American thought from the beginning.[17]

When taken together, these traditions provided a philosophical foundation out of which developed an ethical expression in America for human conduct besieged by the harsh struggle against an unfathomable wilderness and anguished by a distant yet malignant political tyranny. The notion of a continuous universe infinitely expanding according to constant laws of nature and subject to each individual's sense and understanding resulted in the belief in the dignity of the individual who should be free to exercise reason in coming to understand and to act according to the natural law common to all human beings. Through experiment and the power of reason, each individual would enlighten himself or herself as to the constant truths of the universe. In turn, this knowledge would provide the incontestable grounds to shake off the illegitimate fetters of corrupt political and social tradition, leading to a freer and more unified society, a society in which individuals forged a self-government in keeping with the laws of nature. Thus, the optimistic belief in universal law, in the importance of individuals and freely exercised intelligence, and in progress became the chief tenets in the working hypothesis of democracy handed down with faith to 19th Century America.[18]

By way of his Hegelian and rationalist inheritance, Dewey's earliest philosophical work took aim at the handed down metaphysical and epistemological dualisms that work through human conduct to preclude a flourishing democratic experience. Furthermore, this philosophical legacy led Dewey to underscore human beings' responsibility to conceptualize a common good as they act according to the demands within their everyday experience. And as Dewey's interest in physiological psychology grew, he began to work out the human body as the seat of this amelioristic ability. Now, in light of Dewey's philosophical inheritance, does this ability refer to an organic power of human beings to develop themselves and their environment according to the changing and precarious circumstances bearing upon them? If yes, then in what sense does this concept of power entail the ability to control and manipulate other human beings? Or does this ability refer to the power of self-development determined, however, as Dewey's critics claim, by some force transcending human experience but working itself out through the individual's psycho-physiological make-up? In order to see if Dewey simply transferred the handed-down dualisms into psycho-physiological terms, thus leaving him with an insufficient concept of power, it is necessary to work out the details of his response to these dualisms as handed down to him. Getting a clearer understanding of Dewey's direction within this philosophical legacy will provide the foundation to begin tracing out his concept of power in greater detail.

NOTES

[1] John Dewey, "From Absolutism to Experimentalism," *John Dewey, The Later Works, 1925-1953*, vol. 5, edited by Jo Ann Boydston (Carbondale: Southern Illinois University Press, 1984): pp. 154-155.

[2] Bruce Kuklick, The Rise of American Philosophy (New Haven: Yale University Press, 1977): pp. 10-21.

[3] Thomas Reid, *The Philosophical Works of Thomas Reid,* vol. 1, eighth edition, edited and supplemented by Sir William Hamilton (Edinburgh: James Thin, 1803): p.127. Reid writes, "Thus,

the wisdom of philosophy is set in opposition to the common sense of mankind. The first pretends to demonstrate, a priori, that there can be no such thing as a material world; that sun, moon, stars, and earth, vegetable and animal bodies, are, and can be nothing else, but sensations in the mind, or images of those sensations in the memory and imagination; that, like pain and joy, they can have no existence when they are not thought of. The last can conceive no otherwise of this opinion, than as a kind of metaphysical lunacy, and concludes that too much learning is apt to make men mad" *(p. 127).*

[4] Reid, *The Philosophical Works of Thomas Reid*, vol. 1, p. 206. Reid points out that the way to avoid the epistemological deficiencies of both the empiricists' and the rationalists' thought "is to admit the existence of what we see and feel as a first principle, as well as the existence of things whereof we are conscious; and to take our notions of the qualities of body, from the testimony of our senses, with the Peripatetics; and our notions of our sensations, from the testimony of consciousness, with the Cartesians" (p. 206).

[5] Reid, *The Philosophical Works of Thomas Reid*, vol. 1, pp. 245-275; pp. 339-360.

[6] Reid, *The Philosophical Works of Thomas Reid*, vol. 2, eighth edition, edited and supplemented by Sir William Hamilton (Edinburgh: James Thin, 1803): pp. 513-599.

[7] Bruce Kuklick claims that the Scots held to a natural realism that left their metaphysical position unclear (*The Rise of American Philosophy;* New Haven: Yale University Press, 1977; p. 17). Reid states, however, that whatever is beyond human comprehension should be left to the Maker of human kind: "As to the manner how we conceive universals, I confess my ignorance. I know not how I hear, or see, or remember, and as little do I know how I conceive things that have not existence. In all our original faculties, the fabric and manner of operation is, I apprehend, beyond our comprehension, and perhaps is perfectly understood by him only who made them" (*The Philosophical Works of Thomas Reid*, vol. 1; pp. 407-408). Furthermore, Reid says that the extent of the human powers consists in the abilities to give motions to body and direction to thought. "Were we to examine minutely into the connection between our volitions, and the direction of our thoughts which obeys these volitions –were we to consider how we are able to give attention to an object for a certain time, and turn our attention to another when we choose, we might perhaps find it difficult to determine whether the mind itself be the sole efficient cause of the voluntary changes in the direction of our thoughts, or whether it requires the aid of other efficient causes. . . . In both cases, I apprehend, the dispute is endless, and if it could be brought to an issue, would be fruitless. Nothing appears more evident to our reason, than that there must be an efficient cause of every change that happens in nature. But when I attempt to comprehend the manner in which an efficient cause operates, either upon body or upon mind, there is a darkness which my faculties are not able to penetrate" (*The Philosophical Works of Thomas Reid,* vol. 2; pp. 528-529).

[8] William Hamilton, "Editor's Supplementary Dissertations,*"* *The Philosophical Works of Thomas Reid*, vol. 2, pp. 743-988. See pp. 804-815 for Hamilton's development of presentative knowledge as distinguished from representative knowledge. As Hamilton states it, "But Reid's doctrine in this respect is perhaps imperfectly developed, rather than deliberately wrong; and I am confident that had it been proposed to him, he would at once have acquiesced in the distinction of presentative and representative knowledge. . .not only as true in itself, but as necessary to lay a solid foundation for a theory of intuitive perception, in conformity with the common sense of mankind" (p. 813).

[9] Hamilton, "Editor's Supplementary Dissertations," *The Philosophical Works of Thomas Reid*, vol. 2, pp. 881-882.

[10] Herbert Schneider, *A History of American Philosophy* (New York: Columbia University Press, 1946): pp. 246-257.

[11] Kuklick, *The Rise of American Philosophy*, pp. 16-27.

[12] Immanuel Kant, *Kant Selections*, edited by Theodore M. Greene (New York: Charles Scribner's Sons, 1929,1957): pp. 26-29.

[13] Kant, *Kant Selections*, pp. 77-87. According to Kant, "For it is the one consciousness which unites the manifold that has been perceived successively, and afterwards reproduced into one representation. This consciousness may often be very faint, and we may connect it with the effect

only, and not with the act itself, i.e. with the production of a representation. But in spite of this, that consciousness, though deficient in pointed clearness, must always be there, and without it, concepts, and with them, knowledge of objects are perfectly impossible. . . . But the consciousness of oneself, according to the determinations of our state, is, with all our internal perceptions, empirical only, and always transient. There can be no fixed or permanent self in that stream of internal phenomena. It is generally called the internal sense, or the empirical apperception. What is necessarily to be represented as numerically identical with itself, cannot be thought as such by means of empirical data only. It must be a condition which precedes all experience, and in fact renders it possible, for thus only could such a transcendental supposition acquire validity. . . . No knowledge can take place in us, no conjunction or unity of one kind of knowledge with another, without that unity of consciousness which precedes all data of intuition, and without reference to which no representation of objects is possible. This pure, original, and unchangeable consciousness I shall call transcendental apperception" (pp. 77-78).

[14] Georg Wilhelm Friedrich Hegel, *Encyclopedia of Philosophy*, translated and annotated by Gustav Emil Mueller (New York: Philosophical Library, Inc., 1959). Hegel suggests that "the Absolute is simply there in every material or ideal, temporal or non-temporal reality. It is the origin of its presence and of its absence. In every moment it balances being and nothing, beginning and unbeginning, arising and vanishing. It is determined to be there and not to be there. It steps forth in simple unity with itself, but cannot arrest its step" (p. 105). What this implies for the nature of human existence, then, is this: "Universal Being discloses itself in the qualitative infinity of existing moments. Reflecting on this result, it is found in thought that all Being is a dialectical unity of opposites. This essence of all Being discloses itself in actual existences. . . . Reflecting still further again on the movement from Being to Essence and from Essence to Concept, it is evident that the Absolute is the movement or process of self-realization, and that this process of self-realization culminates in the logic of philosophy, which is the logic of world-itself. World-totality as eternal movement in and for itself is the absolute Idea or final cause" (p. 147). For an understanding of how Hegel sees the Absolute working through the human body, see pp. 222-227.

[15] Hegel, *Encyclopedia of Philosophy*, pp. 133-143.

[16] Schneider, *A History of American Philosophy*, pp. 177-193.

[17] Kuklick, *The Rise of American Philosophy*, pp. 10-21. See also Schneider's *A History of American Philosophy* and Ralph Henry Gabriel's *The Course of American Democratic Thought*, second edition (New York: The Ronald Press Company, 1956).

[18] Gabriel, *The Course of American Democratic Thought*, pp. 12-25.

THE ROOTS OF DEWEY'S PRACTICAL PHILOSOPHY

As Morton White has pointed out, there were two distinct lines of intellectual interest that influenced John Dewey's early philosophic development at Johns Hopkins University. One was the philosophy of Hegel, encouraged by Dewey's mentor George S. Morris, a staunch antagonist to British empiricism and the spiritual skepticism that the British –as he saw it—made possible. According to White, it was Morris who provided Dewey with a sense of philosophic friend and foe, handing over to him Hegelian concepts such as "universal consciousness," "self-consciousness," and "organicism" as means to attack British dualisms and to counteract its debilitating ethics. The other intellectual influence on Dewey was physiological and experimental psychology, taught to him by G. Stanley Hall. From his studies with Hall, Dewey came to understand thought as one aspect among several in the homogenous nervous activity of the human organism adjusting to its environment. The findings of physiological psychology gave Dewey a detailed, scientific account for his Hegelian-arrived-at notion that human thought develops organically from within an individual's circumstances. The conclusions of the new psychology, though, made the Hegelian idea of a transcendent Absolute ambiguous at best and downright meaningless at worst. According to White, Dewey eventually would have to find an adequate resolution to the counterclaims of these two interests.[1]

By the time Dewey finished his doctoral work in 1884, however, he had inherited a set of philosophical problems and assumptions out of which his practical philosophy developed and that implicitly entailed a conception of power signifying the individual's ability to direct his or her own self-development, including the enhancement and degradation of the self-development of others. Therefore, to begin getting clearer about Dewey's idea of power, it first is necessary to work out a detailed account of how Dewey employs the assumptions and concepts from Hegel and the findings from physiological psychology in order to mend the dualisms handed down to him. This account will provide a sufficient foundation from which to build an understanding of Dewey's philosophical growth and his idea of power as it is embedded within that growth.

DEWEY'S HEGELIAN ROOTS

It was through his studies with Morris that Dewey came to take up the attack the dualism between mind and matter that was deeply rooted in the empiricist tradition. As Morris saw it, the empiricists failed to account for the power of the human mind, leaving individuals passive, spiritless forms subject to the aimlessness of pure matter. According to Morris, an adequate epistemological account must see the human mind as an active capacity of a particular self attempting to integrate its various circumstances into a unified, ideal whole. The power of the mind serves as the essential means whereby human beings come to realize themselves as organic parts of a larger ideal (the Hegelian Absolute) and thus is the essence of their spiritual and ethical nature.[2] At least up through "Psychology as Philosophic Method," published in 1886, Dewey carried on Morris's Hegelian attack with one important difference. Dewey attempted to fortify his Hegelian concepts with the details from physiological psychology.

Even before Dewey came under the influence of Morris at Johns Hopkins, he had stated what he took to be the problem with locating the seat of knowledge inside material phenomena, as the empiricists had done.

What is materialism? It is the theory which declares that matter and its forces adequately account for all phenomena –those of the material world, commonly so called, and those of life, mind, and society. It declares that not only the content of mind, but that which we call mind itself, is determined by matter. . . .The laws of matter are therefore the laws of mind. Mental phenomena are expressible in terms of material. And since all material phenomena are expressible in terms of the atom and molecule (or whatever names be given to the ultimate forms of matter), therefore all mental are similarly expressible. The ultimate form of matter contains, then, implicitly, all phenomena of mind and society. In short, the coarsest form of matter with which you can begin, as well as the highest organism with which you end, must contain all emotion, volition, and knowledge, the knowing subject and its relations. Beginning, then, with a strictly monistic theory, and keeping directly in line of materialistic reasoning, we have ended with the conclusion that the ultimate form of matter has dualistic "mind" and "matter" properties. Nor is there any escape from this conclusion on a materialistic basis. Therefore on its physical or constructive side we find such a theory suicidal.[3]

According to Dewey, the empiricist metaphysical stance is suicidal because it rests upon a two-world dualism that necessitates a conception of mind that is much more active and constructive than the one the empiricists develop. That is, the empiricist metaphysical account rests upon the idea that all definite relations of meaning, including those of cause-effect relations, lay inherently in the bits and pieces of phenomena. According to the empiricist epistemological account, human beings can come to know these relations of meaning only through the effects of material phenomena impressed upon the human sensory organs, which includes the brain. Since the human mind is a function of the brain and sensory organs (all material phenomena), it is, then, merely a material effect dependent upon matter for its cause and existence. Therefore, as Dewey points out, the empiricist conception of mind as a mere effect or phenomena dependent upon the effects of physical matter fails to account for how it is that the human mind can get behind these apparent qualities of matter in order to know that definite relations of meaning are inherent in this matter. At best, the empiricist account of the mind amounts to nothing more than a random succession of mental phenomena. If the mind functions as a passive sponge absorbing matter as it comes in, then the mind is not capable of producing or constructing an abstraction about the very matter upon which it is dependent for its simple function. Therefore, in order for the empiricists to construct a theory at all testifies to an idea of mind that is active and constructive. As Dewey puts it, "To have real knowledge of real being, there must be something which abides through the successive states, and which perceives their relations to that being and to itself. To say that the mind, if itself a mere phenomena or group of phenomena, can transcend phenomena and obtain a knowledge of that reality which accounts both for other phenomena and for itself, is absurd."[4]

Not all of those from the empiricist tradition, however, held such a simplistic notion of the human mind. By the late 1780s, Thomas Reid had developed a conception of mind as an active human capacity that enables human beings to perceive and conceptualize the apparent qualities of matter in order to adjust their conduct to meet the particular demands within their experience. Reid's idea of mind did not refer to any human power that could penetrate a super experiential realm laying behind and causing the experienced world. Mind, to Reid, was an active human capacity continuous with the rest of the human nervous system and therefore ineluctably conditioned by particular circumstances. The moral implication of Reid's epistemological account was similar to the implications that followed from later findings of biological evolution in the early to mid 1800s: the human organism determining itself in reference to its organic relations with an environment. However, to Sir William Hamilton, Reid's idea of a spatio-temporally conditioned intelligence was itself an assertion of a universal claim in which "there is no cause which is not itself merely an effect, existence being only a series of determined antecedents and determined consequents."[5] Hamilton suggested that Reid's idea of the mind denied the possibility in a transcending moral order working through the universe, therefore denying the existence of God and, in effect, stranding human beings in fatalism.

In order to avoid the destructive implications of Reid's account, Hamilton asserted a world of primary qualities that lay behind and caused the apparent qualities mediated through finite experience. However, because the human ability to know always is conditioned by particular space and time, individuals have no way to know the unconditioned, primary qualities except as these qualities may be intiuted or felt to be behind the apparent world. Thus, Hamilton attempted to preserve a universal moral order on the basis of a metaphysical realm claimed to be independent of human experience and unable to be directly known.

To Dewey, what Hamilton attempted to do was to reconcile metaphysical realism with epistemological relativism, an attempt that rests upon logical contradiction and ends in dualism between mind and matter.[6] On the one hand, Hamilton assumed a realm of unconditioned, primary qualities known only through intuition, which is to say sensation, since intuition refers to some human power other than reason, feeling or sensation being the only human ability left. This amounts to metaphysical realism. On the other hand, Hamilton maintained that these primary qualities of phenomena are the real causes of their apparent qualities that are perceived and conceptualized by the human being responding to particular circumstance. Thus, knowledge of the primary qualities is not definite knowledge of their unconditioned, pure nature but is knowledge of these qualities as they appear relative to the human nervous system. This is what Hamilton called the relativity of knowledge.

Now, according to Dewey, metaphysical realism, taken by itself, is inadequate. It contains the idea that knowledge of the independent realm is derived solely from sensation, which is dependent upon the apparent effects of matter and therefore has no way to infer beyond these apparent effects, unless some sort of constructive mind is asserted. Furthermore, even if an absolute realm independent of experience is admitted for the time being, the theory of the relativity of knowledge itself proves inadequate in getting at it. That is, the theory fails to provide the means necessary to get beyond the spatial and temporal conditions relative to the human nervous system. As Dewey suggests, the matter is not at all improved by developing these stances together, as Hamilton had done.

> We must admit that there is knowledge of the existence of an absolute object. But how is this knowledge obtained? Since all knowledge comes from feeling, this must also. In other words, since sensation-knowledge we must have sensation that there is an absolute existence. But on this theory (that every feeling is relative) an absolute sensation is a contradiction in terms. We may give up the sensationalist hypothesis, and admitting that we have knowledge not derived from feeling (viz., that an Absolute exists), hold that feeling is relative. Or we may give up the Relativity theory and hold, so far at least as this point is concerned, that Sensationalism is true. But to attempt to hold them together is suicidal. If all our knowledge comes from feeling, since we can never have a feeling of the absolute object, we can never have knowledge of it; and we cannot have a feeling of it, since, by the theory, the Absolute is precisely that which is not conditioned by feeling. Or, on the other hand, if we know that all feeling is relative, we do know that there is an absolute object, and hence have knowledge not derived from sensation. When these alternatives are once fairly faced, it will be seen that one or the other must de definitely adopted. Both cannot be accepted.[7]

It is by default, then, that both metaphysical realism and the theory of relative knowledge assume and affirm an active mind. And although Hamilton smuggled in an idea of intuition as the faculty that links a conditioned being with the unconditioned realm, this idea of intuition proves insufficient, since it must refer to some human capacity other than reason if it is to have any meaning at all, and this remaining capacity only can be feeling or sensation. The upshot of this epistemological stance is that it rests knowledge of the unconditioned merely on feeling, which not only contradicts the theory of relative knowledge but also assumes an active mind in order to make such an inference about the unconditioned realm, since feeling has been shown to be inadequate as the sole basis of knowledge. Thus, Dewey shows that Hamilton's theory of relative knowledge assumes, in effect, a human consciousness consisting of sensation and active thought.

According to Dewey, a theory of relative knowledge that includes this idea of consciousness holds correct as a psychological theory. That is, to have knowledge of an external world requires some sort of human consciousness that is in relation to phenomena located in a definite space and time. This consciousness entails both sensation and thought. However, Dewey points out that to argue from this idea of consciousness as a means to prove the existence of an unconditioned absolute which, on the basis of Hamilton's account, must remain absolutely incomprehensible and unknown is logically impossible and meaningless. To have feeling of something as definite requires definite effects in order to stimulate the human nervous system. In this sense, to have a feeling that a world beyond the apparent one exists is to be conscious of something, to sense and think about something definite from which such an inference may be made. Therefore, to have a feeling about something said to exist, yet to be absolutely incomprehensible and unknown, makes no sense, as Dewey states.

> When it is said that something is, it is meant that something is. The predication must be of something; it cannot be of a pure Non-entity, like the Unknowable. The subject must mean something before it can be said either to be or not to be, or have any other intelligible proposition regarding it made. . . . To say that something beyond consciousness is known to exist, is merely to say that the same thing is and is not in consciousness. Its special characteristic is to be out of consciousness; but, so far as it is known to exist, it is in and for consciousness. To suppose otherwise is to suppose that consciousness can in some way get outside of or "beyond" itself, and be conscious of that which is not in consciousness –a proposition as absurd as that a man can stand on his own shoulders, or outstrip his shadow.[8]

As Dewey implies here, a known world must develop as such out of a natural, living relationship with a human consciousness that senses and thinks this world.[9] Therefore, the nature of this knowledge is what the world in all of its parts is experienced as, what it is felt and thought to be. Thus, Dewey resolves the dualism between mind and matter as it comes out of the empiricist epistemological stance: knowledge is relative to a concrete self who is conscious of its surroundings.

So far so good. But, Dewey faces another problem, one that he inherits from within the rationalist tradition. The organic relationship between a known phenomenal world and a human consciousness entails not only the idea that the phenomenal world is dependent upon a finite consciousness for its meaning but also the idea that a finite consciousness depends upon the phenomenal world in order to stimulate it into its meaning-making function. Now, on the basis of Kant's and Hegel's metaphysical accounts, this meaning comes from an unconditioned realm independent of but working through human consciousness. If, as Dewey had shown, it is unwarranted to assume an unconditioned world of meaning transcending human experience, then Kant's universal categories and Hegel's Absolute have no meaning as realms transcending human experience. If the assumption of an unconditioned realm of meaning is dropped, then the problem for Dewey is to account for how human consciousness comes to give meaning and unity to its various finite experiences. Simply put, how is it that individuals have the ability to perceive and conceptualize the bits and pieces of matter relative to their consciousness before this matter affects their nervous systems? How is it that human beings can recognize the effects of a phenomenal world as already imbued with meaning?

In a sense, this problem is the same one that Kant faced in his attempt to account for the mind's ability to synthesize a series of sensory impressions into a continuous and unified flow of activity. Dewey cannot attribute this human ability to some source existing outside of experience. However, Dewey's assumption of the Hegelian tradition seems to suggest that he does assume an unconditioned realm of meaning independent of but working through a concrete consciousness. As he states the problem and solution in "The Psychological Standpoint," "The problem is to reconcile the undoubted relativity of all existence as known, to consciousness, and the undoubted dependence of our own consciousness. . . . The solution is that the consciousness to which all existence is relative is not our consciousness, and that our consciousness is itself relative to consciousness in general."[10]

But Dewey understands that the meaning of "consciousness in general" must be determined by a finite consciousness, which is to say that this meaning must be determined like any other object relative to a particular human being. According to Dewey's account, when an individual attempts to determine the meaning of a consciousness in general, he or she can see only two things: his or her own consciousness as it is ineluctably involved in his or her body's adjustment to his or her particular circumstances and the consciousness of others as manifested in their actions as well. Therefore, "consciousness in general" simply refers to the fact that human consciousness is a process of adjustment.

We are to determine the nature of everything, subject and object, individual and universal, as it is found within conscious experience. Conscious experience testifies, in the primary aspect, my individual self is a "transition," is a process of becoming. But it testifies also that this individual self is conscious of the transition, that it knows the process by which it has become. In short, the individual self can take the universal self as its standpoint, and thence know its own origin. In doing so, it knows that it has its origin in processes which exist for the universal self, and that therefore the universal self never has become. . . . Consciousness is the self-related. Stated from the positive side, consciousness has shown that it involves within itself a process of becoming, and that this process becomes conscious of itself. This process is the individual consciousness; but, since it is conscious of itself, it is consciousness of the universal consciousness. All consciousness, in short, is self-consciousness, and the self is the universal consciousness, for which all process is and which, therefore, always is. The individual consciousness is but the process of realization of the universal consciousness through itself. Looked at as process, as realizing, it is individual consciousness; looked at as produced or realized, as conscious of the process, that is, of itself, it is universal consciousness.[11]

Dewey implies here that the bits and pieces of matter get their significance as they are relative to a conscious being in the process of adjusting to its environment. In turn, this particular conscious being itself is relative to "consciousness in general," which, again, means the process of adjustment by human beings in general. Now, according to Dewey, to realize that one's conscious activity is like the activity of all other human consciousness is to realize a few things. First, it is to realize that one is a part of a larger whole, that is, a part of human consciousness in general, a union of spirits in a sense. This is what Dewey calls taking the standpoint of the universal self. Second, it is to realize that, by virtue of being a part of human consciousness in general, one's particular conscious activity, one's particular process of adjustment, is the kind of activity in which human beings in general might engage. Furthermore, this implies that the activities of others are possibilities for oneself. Therefore, Dewey employs "universal consciousness" to refer to the unity of all processes by which human beings adjust themselves to their environments.

As Dewey argues four months later in "Psychology as Philosophic Method," this universal consciousness, this unity of all processes, has no existence and no meaning except as realized by a human consciousness, which always is a particular human consciousness, a specific self who is attending to his or her circumstances.[12] That is, when the individual takes the standpoint of the universal self, he or she can see for certain, as absolute, that there are processes that exist for human beings in general but that these processes depend upon a particular self in order to be put into effect and realized. This is what Dewey calls "the absolute self-consciousness," since, as he says, all consciousness, including universal consciousness, is self-consciousness.

What is this distinction between the absolute self-consciousness and its manifestation in a being like man? Is the absolute self-consciousness complete in itself, or does it involve this realization and manifestation in a being like man? If it is complete in itself, how can any philosophy which is limited to "this absolute principle of self-consciousness" face and solve the difficulties involved in its going beyond itself to manifest itself in self-consciousness? This cannot be what is meant. The absolute self-consciousness must involve within itself, as organic member of its very being and activity, this manifestation and revelation. Its being must be this realization and manifestation. Granted that this realization and manifestation is an act not occurring in time, but eternally completed in the nature of the Absolute, and that it occurs only "partially" and "interruptedly" through (not in) time, in a being like man.[13]

On the basis of the relativity of knowledge, an individual's particular experience is always conditioned by his or her particular context. Therefore, it is logical to assume when Dewey says that an individual realizes the Absolute "partially" and "interruptedly," he means that an individual's awareness of the Absolute is circumscribed always by his or her temporal, finite nature and must remain an incomplete awareness that develops according to the quality and quantity of his or her experiences in the world. In the same article, however, Dewey maintains that although an individual may be characterized as finite, he "has manifested in him the unity of all being and knowing, and is not finite, i.e., an object or event, but is, in virtue of his self-conscious nature, infinite, the bond, the living union of all objects and events."[14] Since, according to Dewey, self-consciousness (or being in any intelligible sense) has its origin in the processes that are for human consciousness in general, what "the unity of all being and knowing" refers to here is simply these processes, universal consciousness or Absolute. But, what does Dewey mean when he says that the human being has the unity of these processes manifested in him or her? He cannot mean that all of these processes are innate in a single human mind or that the individual somehow can experience the unity of these processes in a completed form at any one time. To maintain such as this is to contradict the theory of relative knowledge, and Dewey has shown that the theory of relative knowledge is inescapable on all epistemological accounts. Thus, universal consciousness as a concept that refers to the unity of all human processes which can be realized in its entirety by an individual at any one time is superfluous, as Morton White has noted, because an individual's awareness of these processes can develop only partially and relatively according to the demands of his or her particular context.[15] Although Dewey is not explicit in his development of universal consciousness as a realizable unity, it is warranted to assume that universal consciousness as unity expresses a moral ideal instead of a metaphysical fact, particularly in light of the influence of physiological psychology on Dewey's thought.

THE INFLUENCE OF PHYSIOLOGICAL PSYCHOLOGY ON DEWEY'S HEGELIAN IDEALISM

In "Soul and Body," an article published within the same month as "Psychology as Philosophic Method," Dewey employs findings from physiological psychology in order to underscore thought as an organic part within the nervous process of the human organism, the overall function of which is the adjustment of this organism to meet the demands of its environment.[16] Characterizing this nervous activity as such, Dewey suggests that, while all human nervous activity is a process of adjustment in form, the meaning of this process in terms of its direction and effects is dependent upon the particulars bearing down upon the organism. On the basis of his idea that the meaning of this adjustment depends upon context, Dewey makes the case that this meaning is not innate to the human being but is acquired and learned. Now, what are the findings from physiological psychology as Dewey understands them and how do these facts lead him towards the conclusion that the processes of adjustment are learned activities?

There are a few important facts from physiological investigations about the psycho-physiological composition of the human organism. First, according to Dewey, is the fact that the entire nervous system of the organism is composed of fibers and cells. As Dewey understands it, fibers and cells are of like chemical compounds and have complementary functions. Fibers transfer stimuli from sensory receptors to a collection of cells (nerve centers) and back to sensory receptors or from one nerve center to another. The cell takes in this stimuli and reacts to it by releasing its own stored up energy either to inhibit the incoming stimuli from continued conduction or to direct its continued conduction. Since the brain is composed of fibers and cells similar to the rest of the nervous system, its function, therefore, is similar: to transfer, inhibit, and control. Insofar as the brain is associated with thought or mental processes, according to Dewey, then thought is not only similar in kind to the rest of the nervous system but is inherent in it throughout.

The psychical is homogeneously related to the physiological. Whatever the relation of the psychical to the neural, it is related in the same manner to all parts of the neural. The brain is no more the organ of the mind than the spinal cord, the spinal cord no more than the peripheral endings of the nerve fibres. The brain is undoubtedly most closely and most influentially connected with the life of the soul, but its connection is of the same kind as that of every other part of the nervous system. Now this gives us but one alternative: either there is absolutely no connection between the body and soul at any point whatever, or else the soul is, through the nerves, present to all the body. This means that the psychical is immanent in the physical. To deny this is to go back to the Cartesian position, and make a miracle of the whole matter –to call in some utterly foreign power to make the transition which is actually found.[17]

The second important finding from physiological psychology is that the stimulation and reaction of the nervous system is a process of adjustment, the particular nature or character of which develops according to specific environmental pressures. As Dewey points out, the nervous tissue consists of a highly volatile chemical compound that becomes unbalanced when disturbed by stimuli. In order to return this chemical material back to its resting state, the cell responds by releasing its own stored-up energy in an amount necessary to achieve this resting state. However, as Dewey notes, if there was no resistance to and regulation of the exciting energy by the cell, the organism would respond to every stimulus until its potential or stored energy was exhausted. Thus, the function of the cell is one of control such that the incoming stimulus is met with sufficient energy. This cellular energy works either to inhibit the progress of the stimulus all together or to modify its intensity so that the resting state of the neural compound is restored, reserve energy is not used up completely, and energy generated from this reaction itself is stored for potential use. Since the human body may be affected in numerous ways by an infinite range of stimuli, it requires a complex collection of cells, or nerve centers, connected and working together not only to secure the organism with reference to the immediate stimulus but to develop it for future ends. As Dewey concludes, "The psychical is immanent in the physical; immanent as directing it towards an end, and for the sake of this end selecting some activities, inhibiting others, responding to some, controlling others, and adjusting and co-ordinating the complex whole, so as, in the simplest and least wasteful way, to reach the chosen end."[18]

According to Dewey, since particular stimuli affect particular nerve centers in the body, the process of adjustment to this stimuli becomes more defined in these nerve centers and their helper centers. Borrowing the phrase from physiology, this is what Dewey calls the "localization of function," which, again, simply means that the particular process of adjustment in the immediately affected nerve centers creates the capacity and tendency in these centers to act or perform in a similar way in the future. The degree to which these particular functions are defined in the nerve centers depends directly upon how necessary these functions or adjustments are to the maintenance of life in the organism. For example, breathing, blinking, swallowing, temperature control, digesting, and excreting are the more simpler but fundamental house-keeping functions of the organism which have more developed locations of control in specific nerve centers. The higher or more complex functions such as walking, writing, and speaking require a large number of coordinated nerve centers and have less definition of location in any one spot than the more vital functions. Therefore, the function of ideas, the coordination of nerve centers for the further development of the organism along the tendencies already formed in the body, has no specific location of control at all but requires a vast connection of numerous nerve centers. Thus, on the basis of this physiological fact, Dewey argues that the higher functions, including those of ideas and meaning, are not innate to any specific neurological cells but are developed or acquired through the continued process of adjustment to particular stimuli.

> The two statements already made that localization is practically universal, and yet that the higher intellectual powers cannot be definitely localized at all, do not contradict each other. They find their reconciliation in the statement that localization is not original, but acquired. It has already been stated that localization is no quality inherent in the cell; but that it depends upon the cell's connections through its fibres. . . . And this dependence of localized function upon connection, is the same as to say that given elements of the brain act in a certain way only because they have been associated in the performance of the act. The localization is dependent upon use and exercise. . . . Localization of function is, in short, only the physiological way of saying habit. The organization of function is not indwelling in the brain as so much matter: it has been learned by the brain and learned through the tuition and care of the soul.[19]

Given these psycho-physiological facts, then, the only intelligible ideal for the soul is the further enhancement of the soul's processes of adjustment such that these processes become ever more defined and perfect not only in themselves but in their connections with each other as the unified mechanism whereby the soul can go on to further develop itself. Simply put, the ideal for the soul is the further realization of itself as manifested in its body.[20] Now, in light of Dewey's understanding of the facts from physiological psychology, his idea of universal consciousness as the expression of a moral ideal should become clearer. When Dewey writes that the human being "has manifested in him the unity of all being and knowing" and is "infinite," he simply means that by virtue of having a soul, a consciousness that adjusts, the human being is connected to all like beings -- including those past, present, and future-- who possess this ability to adjust to and therefore know the world. Dewey simply is expressing the idea that by virtue of this connection, the individual is a social being who has the potential to realize and enrich the meaning of those processes taken up by others who have come before and for those who will come after. The particular processes that an individual takes up provide the conditions for thought such that he or she not only comes to determine the significance of phenomena in the course of carrying out the processes but comes to see his or her consciousness as a particular realization of the kind of activity that human beings in general might realize. In short, the particular processes that are given individual form are the basis through which an individual comes to understand himself or herself as a particular self, that is, as the kind of person who engages in this or that type of activity.

Since phenomena and the empirical self are defined on the basis of particular processes taken up by a conscious self, the highest form of human knowledge is self-knowledge. Since self-knowledge is directly proportional to the quality and quantity of processes taken up, then the highest moral ideal is the further expression and realization of oneself as manifested through the universal processes of adjustment. Because the particular self always takes up processes that are for and by human beings in general, the moral ideal of self realization serves the greater, more universal good by expanding the meaning of the specific processes assumed and therefore expanding the possibilities for further human experience in general. This implies, then, that it is human beings who ultimately have the responsibility to determine and realize a common good as they act according to the particular demands on their experience. Furthermore, since the processes of adjustment are learned, the ideal of self realization entails the social obligation to cultivate those processes in one another that lead each to the further expression of himself or herself and to a fuller appreciation for his or her connection to others. This cultivation is what Dewey means by "the tuition and care of the soul." Thus, it is from within the human struggle to achieve this ideal of self realization, according to Dewey, that philosophy develops as the process by which individuals become conscious of themselves as universal selves who carry out the universal processes of adjustment.

Drawing on Hegel, Dewey suggests that the Absolute is "a unity which lives through its distinctions."[21] That is, the human experience of the processes of adjustment is one of necessary difference between these processes. If differences between these processes were not experienced, then there would be no need to distinguish one process from another and thus no need for concepts and ideas. There would be no need for individuals to distinguish themselves as those who carry out these different processes. Since each individual's experience is a partial realization of the Absolute, and since this partial realization presupposes some realization of the Absolute that is different, differences and conflicts within and between individuals' experiences are inevitable. Now, according to Dewey, philosophy emerges as a process among all others in which the individual becomes conscious of himself or herself as one who takes up the universal processes.[22] More specifically, philosophy is that mode of thought by which the individual comes to locate the conflicts within the Absolute as these conflicts are manifested through him or her in the particular. This is what Dewey calls the analytic function of philosophy, the breaking down of experience into its constituent parts in order to determine the significance of each in its bearing upon the meaning of the whole. But, philosophy also has the conceptual task of modifying these conflicting processes such that these conflicts are resolved and the processes are integrated more completely. This is what Dewey calls the synthetic function of philosophy, the aim of which is to enable human beings not only to meet the demands of their particular context but in meeting these demands, to realize more fully the meaning of the Absolute as an integration of all human effort and to enrich this meaning with further possibilities.[23] Thus, it is through his assumption of the Hegelian tradition that Dewey first comes to see philosophy as a living process, a special mode of human thought, that develops organically out of the particular conflicts within everyday experience and that aims to reconcile these conflicts so that this experience becomes more complete and rich with meaning.

Moreover, through the Hegelian tradition, Dewey inherits not only the enduring philosophical dualism of mind and matter but also the conceptual means by which to mend this dualism. Dewey's idea of human consciousness as a process consisting of both sense and thought developing according to the external pressures within a particular space and time enables him to maintain that there is no warrant to assume a metaphysical absolute outside of this finite process. According to Dewey, the individual is an active being who comes to know and modify the world and himself or herself in it as the meaning of these things emerge out of a living relationship with his or her finite nature. Since the individual's being is relative always to other human beings as an ontological fact, his or her particular self development is inherently connected to the development of other human beings, including those past, present, and future. Thus, the moral nature of human beings is directly dependent upon their responsibility to define and modify their development in reference to the particular material and social demands on them. Fundamentally, this responsibility entails a self development that leads not only to a more refined and flexible sense of oneself as a conscious being intrinsically connected to others but to the encouragement of this sense in others as well.

HEGELIAN IDEALISM AND THE CONCEPT OF THE BIOLOGICAL ORGANISM

Now this ideal of self-realization implied within Dewey's earliest philosophical work is suggestive of his understanding not only of power but of democracy as well. From the beginning of his philosophical career, Dewey attacked any stance suggesting that human conduct is determined and caused by some force existing outside human experience. On Dewey's account, human beings are equipped with all the capacities or powers of conscious activity necessary to define their own response to environmental demands and to modify this response as these demands change. Therefore, this conscious capacity of people to carry out their particular processes of adjustment with greater understanding, refinement, and flexibility simply means their power of self-realization.

Dewey recognizes, however, that this process of self-realization inherently involves other people and therefore entails inevitable conflict. That is, insofar as human beings come to cross purposes in experience, either they meet the source of conflict such that they continue in their respective purposes with more depth and range of meaning or this source precludes them from regulating their own adjustment to their particular environment. Furthermore, since the processes of adjustment are learned and are, therefore, cultivated responses, it is possible that human beings cultivate those social processes in such a way that has the effect of making the powers of human consciousness rigid in adjustment. Thus, that which arrests or reduces an individual's flexibility to respond to immediate change thereby limits the possible means by which he or she may continue to express and realize himself or herself further as a social being. Therefore, all that diminishes the individual's ability to modify his conduct may be understood to have power over his or her self-realization.

Since, according to Dewey, philosophy emerges out of the particular conflicts within everyday experience, a chief function of philosophy is to break down this experience into its significant parts in order to clarify how these parts work together to impede or to have power over the process of self realization. Simply put, then, Dewey inherits a conception of philosophy that entails an understanding of power as both the ability to have an effect on others and the ability to have an effect over others. The ideal of self realization provides the best standard by which to judge the value of this effect on others as either liberating or restricting and to guide the other chief philosophical task of suggesting ways of mending conflict so that collective experience may grow and flourish. Thus, on the basis of this ideal as worked out in detail from Dewey's epistemological stance, the handed-down tenets of the democratic faith (universal law, individual dignity, and progress) cannot refer to some moral absolute determining human experience from outside of it. What these principles signify are the best working guides that develop from within and are most conducive to the kind of human association that allows individuals to realize for themselves the universal law of process as inherent in their particular being and to determine and enhance the meaning of this process as the means by which to expand their organic connections to each other. In this sense, democracy simply means the ethical ideal of self-realization.

While this ethical ideal, which includes both the power of self-realization and power over self-realization, is implied within Dewey's earliest work, it becomes clearer and more thoroughly worked out as Dewey draws upon the details of physiological psychology. That is, as Dewey increasingly employs neurological facts from psycho-physiological investigations, he is able to account for body and soul as homogeneous parts of the human nervous system and begins to conceptualize human conduct as the process by which the human organism adjusts to its environment. This biological detail, then, lends Dewey a more basic foundation from which to fill out and unify his Hegelian-arrived-at epistemological, social, and ethical insights. Gradually, as Dewey himself points out, his Hegelian language is shed and his practical, experimental philosophy begins to emerge and mature.[24] "Universal consciousness," signifying those shared processes of adjustment, gives way to "habit," construed as social function or practice; "self consciousness," meaning the individual expression of these universal processes, yields to "social intelligence," or habit guided by thought that is self possessive; and the ideal of self realization simply comes to mean faith in a democratic experience. The next few chapters will work out these epistemological, social, and ethical details of Dewey's mature philosophy in order to get a more refined focus on his idea of power.

NOTES

[1] Morton White, *The Origins of Dewey's Instrumentalism* (New York: Octagon Books, Inc., 1943/1964). For the influence of both Morris and Hall on Dewey's early philosophy, see also George Dykhuizen's *The Life and Mind of John Dewey*, introduced by Harold Taylor and edited by Jo Ann Boydston (Carbondale: Southern Illinois University Press, 1973) and Ryan's *John Dewey and The Hide Tide of American Liberalism* (New York: W.W. Norton and Company, 1995).

[2] White, *The Origins of Dewey's Instrumentalism*, pp. 12-33.

[3] John Dewey, "The Metaphysical Assumptions of Materialism," *John Dewey, The Early Works, 1882-1888*, vol. 1, edited by Jo Ann Boydston (Carbondale: Southern Illinois University Press, (1969): pp. 3-4.

[4] Dewey, "The Metaphysical Assumptions of Materialism," *The Early Works*, vol. 1, pp. 5-6.

[5] Hamilton, "Editor's Supplementary Dissertations," *The Philosophical Works of Thomas Reid*, vol. 2, p. 974. For a fuller development Hamilton's objection to the moral implications of Reid's epistemology, see pp. 973-981.

[6] Dewey, "Knowledge and The Relativity of Feeling," *The Early* Works, vol. 1, pp. 19-33.

[7] Dewey, "Knowledge and The Relativity of Feeling," *The Early Works*, vol. 1, p. 23.

[8] Dewey, "Knowledge and The Relativity of Feeling," *The Early Works*, vol. 1, p. 26.

[9] As Dewey puts it, "We are now prepared to draw a positive conclusion and say that the real meaning of the theory of Relativity of Feeling is that a feeling is a specific determinate relation or reaction given in consciousness between two bodies, one a sensitive, the other a non-sensitive object. It is possible to hold it, therefore, in conjunction with a theory which allows knowledge of these objective conditions, the knowledge of their relation as given in feeling, though relative indeed to the subject, is not for that reason a detraction from our knowledge of objects, but rather an addition. . . . Except upon the theory that the real nature of things is their nature out of relation to everything, knowledge of the mode of relation between an object and an organism is just as much genuine knowledge as knowledge of its physical and chemical properties, which in turn are only its relations" (*The Early Works*, vol.1, p. 31).

[10] Dewey, "The Psychological Standpoint," *The Early Works*, vol. 1, pp. 132-133.

[11] Dewey, "The Psychological Standpoint," *The Early Works*, vol. 1, p. 142.

[12] Dewey, "Psychology as Philosophic Method," *The Early Works*, vol. 1, pp.144-167. Put in Dewey's words, "Were not the universe realized in the individual, it would be impossible for the individual to rise to a universal point of view, and hence to philosophize. . . . The universe, except as realized in an individual, has no existence. . . . Self-consciousness means simply an individualized universe" (pp. 148-149).

[13] Dewey, "Psychology as Philosophic Method," *The Early Works*, vol. 1, p. 157.

[14] Dewey, "Psychology as Philosophic Method," *The Early Works*, vol. 1, p. 146.

[15] White, *The Origin of Dewey's Instrumentalism*, p. 47.

[16] Dewey, "Soul and Body," *The Early Works*, vol. 1, pp. 93-115.

[17] Dewey, "Soul and Body," *The Early Works*, vol. 1, p. 96.

[18] Dewey, "Soul and Body," *The Early Works*, vol. 1, p. 100; pp. 93-100. According to Dewey, "In short, there must be something which gives control, which regulates the reaction, and which also ensures a reserve power. There must be opposed to the exciting activity one which resists, and thereby prevents the whole force at hand, the whole unstable compound , from being used, and which also restores it as it is expended. And so it is found that there is a complementary process. Not only is energy being constantly put forth, but energy is being constantly stored up or rendered latent. Not all the force which comes to a nervous element is employed in breaking down the unstable compounds and thereby losing energy; part –in some cases much the greater part—is used in building up these unstable compounds, thereby forming a reservoir of energy for future use, while the process itself acts as a restraint upon, a control over, the excitatory factor. Every nervous action is, therefore, a reciprocal function of stimulation, excitation, and inhibition; control through repression. Every nervous activity is essentially an adjustment" (pp. 97-980).

[19] Dewey, "Soul and Body," *The Early Works*, vol. 1, pp. 110-111.

[20] As Dewey puts it, "By the performance of its acts the soul gains a mechanism by which to perform them again the more readily, economically, and perfectly. . . . The body is not an external instrument which the soul has happened upon, and consequently uses, as a musician might happen upon a piano. The body is the organ of the soul because by the body the soul expresses and realizes its own nature. It is the outward form and living manifestation of the soul" ("Soul and Body," *The Early Works*, vol. 1, p. 112).

[21] Dewey, "Psychology as Philosophic Method," *The Early Works*, vol. 1, p. 166. See also pp. 163-167.

[22] Dewey, "Psychology as Philosophic Method," *The Early Works*, vol. 1, pp. 146-147, 148-149, 152, 154, 163.

[23] Dewey, "Kant and Philosophic Method," *The Early Works*, vol. 1, pp. 42-43. Dewey states that "philosophy comes into existence when men are confronted with problems and contradictions which common sense and the special sciences are able neither to solve nor resolve" (p. 34).

[24] Dewey, "From Absolutism to Experimentalism," *John Dewey, The Later Works, 1925-1953*, vol. 5, edited by Jo Ann Boydston (Carbondale: Southern Illinois University Press, 1984): pp. 154-155.

HABIT: THE SEAT OF DEWEY'S IDEA OF POWER

In *The Promise of Pragmatism*, John Patrick Diggins suggests that Dewey's use of a biological vocabulary to explain the nature of human experience kept Dewey from examining "the depths of motivation" as the origin of human control and manipulation over others.[1] Diggins assumes that because Dewey employed a biological framework, he necessarily saw the human being as an organism evolving through a simple stimulus-response cycle without the mediation of interest, emotion, and thought. Without the ability to account for the subjective side of human behavior, as Diggins implies, Dewey could not account for how and why the human organism comes to control and manipulate its environment, including other human beings. Similarly, C. Wright Mills has pointed out in *Sociology and Pragmatism* that Dewey's biological framework only allowed Dewey to see problems between the organism and its environment, which, in effect, led Dewey to exclude conflicts between human beings as problems to be worked on and, thus, led him to obscure power relations within society.[2]

As pointed out in the previous chapter, however, Dewey sufficiently argued against any philosophical stance suggesting that human action is determined and caused by some force existing outside of human experience. According to Dewey's account, the human organism is endowed with all the capacities of conscious activity necessary to define its own response to environmental demands and to adjust this response as these demands change. Furthermore, this idea that the human organism has the ability to adjust itself to its environment such that it increases the depth, precision, and unity in meaning of its activity entails at least four important implications in Dewey's work. First, it implies that the activities whereby the human being adjusts itself are acquired and developed tendencies or habits directly dependent upon the particular interaction between the human being and environment. Second, since an individual's environment always includes other human beings already engaged in activities aimed at common ends, then any single individual's particular tendencies of action are inextricably social and, thus, are socially learned and cultivated responses. According to Dewey, it is through these shared practices that an individual comes to know the world in its infinite meaning and grows as a self as he or she attempts to realize and enrich this meaning for a common good. Thus, third, these shared practices inherently entail particular common ends to be achieved and, therefore, are the specific means through which individuals come to realize and enhance their connections with each other. In other words, the shared practices as means to particular common goods are all one with what Dewey argued as the more encompassing moral ideal of self-realization. Fourth, as also pointed out at the end of the previous chapter, this ideal of self-realization is suggestive of Dewey's idea of power. That is, individuals' conscious ability to carry out shared practices such that they come to modify themselves through their environment toward increased understanding, refinement, and responsiveness is their power of self-realization. This ability of individuals to act for common ends does not preclude them from coming to cross-purposes such that conflict arrests the human ability to modify conduct so as to increase its depth and range of meaning. Therefore, anything that reduces the human ability to expand the meaning of shared practices may be understood to have power over self-realization.

In order to get a better insight into Dewey's idea of power, it is necessary to work out the ideal of self-realization as it is grounded in Dewey's understanding of the psycho-physiological processes of the human organism. Working out the details of this make-up will provide a foundation necessary to do several things. In this chapter, it will allow for a refined understanding of the nervous activity whereby the human organism consciously adjusts itself in order to get a better and more significant control over its environment. In subsequent chapters, these details will form the basis by which to underscore the organism's native impulses to act as inherently social and, therefore, to point up these tendencies as cultivated social habits. These details also will sharpen the focus on social habit as the means through which individuals come to realize themselves as particular selves attempting to carry out shared purposes for a common good. Thus, working out the psycho-physiological mechanism of habit will illuminate Dewey's idea of power as the ability to act in such a way so as either to expand and invigorate the self or narrow and weaken it. Moreover, this biological framework will help make the point that human beings are always in particular relations of power, the effects of which must be determined through the particular shared practices that they take up in order to meet specific contextual demands. Finally, these biological details will provide the essential foundation from which to trace out Dewey's idea of education as the conscious cultivation of the powers of human adjustment necessary to realize and enrich a democratic experience.

APPERCEPTION AND RETENTION AS THE ESSENTIAL PROCESSES OF HABIT

Throughout his career, Dewey maintained that an external world of material phenomena and an internal one of human feeling are just two ways to distinguish different aspects comprising the homogenous circuit of human consciousness. As pointed out in the last chapter, Dewey argued early in his career against the materialist position that rested upon a rigid separation between consciousness and matter and that reduced consciousness to a mere effect of concrete phenomena. According to Dewey, both feeling that an external world exists and a mind that actively orders this feeling into meaningful sense are necessary to have a continuous, unified experience. Later in his career, Dewey suggested that experience always is one of saturation and coordination between some particular part of nature and a feeling, thinking human being such that both become constituent of and grow out of each other. He said in *Human Nature and Conduct*,

Breathing is an affair of the air as truly as of the lungs; digesting an affair of food as truly as of tissues of stomach. Seeing involves light just as certainly as it does the eye and optic nerve. Walking implicates the ground as well as the legs; speech demands physical air and human companionship and audience as well as vocal organs. . . .The same air that under certain conditions ruffles the pool or wrecks buildings, under other conditions purifies the blood and conveys thought.[3]

The fact of this coordination, moreover, led Dewey to a more detailed and systematic investigation of its particular functions. How is it that the environment is taken into the human organism through the medium of feeling such that it gains an ideal significance and, thus, becomes a psychical stimulus for the organism to act and grow? Though Dewey's particular answer to this question runs throughout all his work, it got its most explicit development in his *Psychology*.[4]

In this work, Dewey suggests that the coordination by which human beings adjust themselves to their environment can be seen in two complementary functions working simultaneously as a single unit: apperception and retention. Apperception refers to the ordering functions of conscious activity (including association, dissociation, and attention) that give significance to sensual material by connecting it with the past experience of the self. It is the means by which the self is brought to bear upon the environment, according to Dewey. Retention, for its part, depends on the ordering functions of apperception but most closely refers to the reverberation that the connected material has on the range and depth of meaning of the self's experience. It is the side of apperception that digests interpreted material into the living tissue of the self such that the material becomes an effect for further, more definite apperception. Apperception, then, is the side of retention that keeps the past experience of the self living by continuously interpreting sensuous material in light of this experience. Put in Dewey's words, "Apperception may be defined, at the outset, as the reaction of mind by means of its organized structure upon the sensuous material presented to it. Retention is the reaction of the apperceived content upon the organized structure of the mind."[5]

Put in the physiological terms of the previous chapter, without the ability of the central nervous system to be somewhat malleable to its own sensory-motor discharge, it would not be capable of retaining the effect of this discharge as a pre-disposition or tendency to act similarly in the future. Without retention, the individual could not develop a nervous structure –let alone an organized structure—that could be called a past experience by which to comprehend sensuous material. If the nervous system were not strong enough to regulate the conduction of stimuli, it would respond to a flood of excitation indiscriminately until it quickly drained itself into a stupor. Without apperception, the individual could not develop an organized nervous structure to coordinate a controlled and continuous response to sensuous material.

Now, according to Dewey, feeling aroused by some physical motion serves as a necessary stimulus for the mind to connect this feeling with the rest of its nervous structure. That is, an external stimulus must produce some change in the peripheral nervous system that acts as a physiological stimulus for its further conduction to the brain. Once in the brain, this change acts as a psychical stimulus for the coordination of a motor adjustment to the stimulus. As Dewey points out, the mind will connect sensuous elements into a continuous experience by associating those elements occurring contiguously in space or time and by combining those having similar prevailing qualities. That is, the mind will integrate a room full of individuals sitting behind desks, for example, into a single idea, a classroom full of students. Or, say, if an infant feels nourished at her mother's breast roughly at the same time that she hears a soft hum, the infant's mind will associate these sensations as elements of a single activity, place, and time. Thus, as Dewey puts the law of association by contiguity, "If various sensory elements, or even ideas, contiguous in place or time, are associated simultaneously in one activity, they become integral portions of it and recur with it."[6] Therefore, the sight of a desk may act as a physical stimulus for the individual to recall a specific room full of particular individuals, along with any particular concomitant sounds or smells. Or, a soft hum might stimulate the infant's feelings to nourish at her mother's breast.

According to Dewey, association by contiguity leads to the development of a higher form of association, that of similarity. In more physiological terms, the sensory-motor discharge coordinated by the mind in response to simultaneously occurring sensations is retained in the nervous system as a predisposition to act similarly in the future. Since the brain regulates its body's nervous energy in order to respond with the fullest coordination possible at the least cost, it attempts to connect or associate an incoming stimulus with some sensory-motor discharge previously formed and retained as part of its nervous structure.[7] This connection or association by similarity, then, enables the mind to respond more efficiently to its environment than if it had to coordinate a response afresh. For example, a novice swimmer who has no experience in the water will expend a massive amount of energy forming a muscle coordination necessary simply to stay afloat. A beginning surfer may exhaust herself simply trying to distribute her weight while lying on her board. However, even though the novice swimmer and surfer have to coordinate new sensory-motor adjustments to new stimuli, the adjustment, once formed, enables these individuals in at least two important ways. These adjustments will be retained and will expand the range of their nervous tendencies to act and, by virtue of this retention, will serve as pathways for them to act more readily and with less waste of energy in the future given similar circumstances. Therefore, insofar as the incoming stimulus induces the mind to respond along an old line of discharge, then it may be said that the incoming stimulus is similar in some prevailing quality to a previously experienced stimulus that induced the same response. Once this connection by similarity is made, the mind has given its original feeling of an external stimulus significance. That is, the mind has made the feeling a sign of a definite existence having a particular relation to some retained effect of a previous discharge. According to Dewey, this relation serves as the mainspring of intellectual life. "If we inquire under what circumstances any object or event enters into our intellectual life as significant, we find that it is when it is connected in an orderly way with the rest of our experience. . . .To be significant is to be a sign; that is, to point to something beyond its own existence to which it is related. . . Relationship is the essence of meaning."[8]

Apperception and retention, then, are the essential processes that not only constitute what Dewey calls the train of ideas but, as such, build up the self-executing mechanism of habit. For example, simply walking into the water serves as a stimulus for the developing swimmer to shift his body into the proper horizontal position necessary to propel himself. This act itself works as a stimulus for additional successive associations for the swimmer to hold his breath and submerge himself, to thrust his legs back and forth in a controlled, alternating pattern, and to push water from front to side with arms extended and hands cupped. Furthermore, as Dewey puts the law of association by similarity, "If any activity has frequently recurred, any element often occurring gains in redintegrating power at the expense of those occurring less often, and will finally gain the power of action independently, so as itself to redintegrate ideas by the law of contiguity."[9] In other words, the more often an activity occurs, the more definite it develops as a sensory-motor coordination. Every movement of the swimmer becomes integrated further with the next movement and induces a more precise and fluid stroke. As this activity matures, the presence of any single element of the complete activity may initiate the execution of the whole, requiring little conscious attention to the particular muscular movements in their proper relation necessary to the end, in this case, planing the water. A reduction in the mental effort required to act upon a retained sensory-motor tendency is what Dewey means when he suggests, as above, that the activity gains the power of independent execution.

The more definite an activity becomes, the stronger it grows as a retained tendency or mechanism by which the individual carries on his or her associating functions. That is, the activity becomes a structure, a pathway, in the nervous system to which the individual can connect incoming stimuli and, thus, give them sense and significance.

In general the function of association in the psychical life is the formation of a mechanism. It serves to connect the various elements of our mental life together by such firm bands that they may be used as a foundation upon which to erect more complex mental structures. It takes isolated sensations and consolidates them. It takes chaotic material and it gives it definite form, consisting of a number of specialized modes of activity. The state of the mind without associations may be compared to a fluid; that on which the associative powers have been at work to this fluid crystallized, thus made into solid forms of positive shape and definite relation to each other. . . .More specifically, all that we call routine or habit, all that is mechanical in the life of the soul, is the result of associative activities. . . .By habit, whether intellectual or volitional, we mean nothing else than such a connection of ideas or acts that, if one be presented, the rest of the series follow without the intervention of consciousness or the will. . . .The object of habit is thus, on the one hand, to create a mechanism which shall attend to the familiar and permanent elements of experience, and, on the other, to leave the conscious activity of mind free to control new and variable factors. . . .It is the centre of gravity of the spiritual world. It is constituted, on the one hand, by the simple facts of family, business, church, and social life; on the other, by the objects which present themselves most regularly, varying with the man of affairs, the artist, and the man of science.[10]

Fundamentally, then, habit is the seat of human power to act in the world. According to Dewey, it is by virtue of the self-executing nature of habit that the human organism gains not only the capacity of physical adjustment with its environment but the ability to render its adjustments more unified and meaningful. The developing muscular coordination of the swimmer, for example, extends his range of interacting with the water by enabling him to move through it at greater depths and lengths than he was able to reach before. Through sheer contiguity with other activities associated with water, the swimmer's range of tendencies or habits may be expanded to include surfing and diving, which further enlarge his relationship with the water. Another way of saying this is that habit is the instrument that develops interest, insofar as "interest" refers to an impulse to act along some retained tendency in response to a feeling aroused by some object so that the object becomes connected to the activity as a particular means to a particular end. Engaging in these new activities, then, the swimmer may develop interest in other dimensions of this particular body of water, including its depth, structure, and aquatic life, that he had never been exposed to before or that he was able to experience at one time only by book. In this latter sense, the original tendency to swim serves as the means through which his activities of surfing and diving grow into and are unified with his other interests, reading and investigating about aquatic ecosystems. Now, confronted by a different body of water, the swimmer will bring his developing tendency to swim as well as his other newly formed habits to bear upon this different stimulus. Thus, this different body of water gains meaning as a sign for the swimmer to act further upon all the possible tendencies that he has developed through his previous experiences in water. Dewey gets closer to making the point that habit is power or effective capacity in *Human Nature and Conduct*:

> All habits are demands for certain kinds of activity; and they constitute the self. In any intelligible sense of the word will, they are will. They form our effective desires and they furnish us with our working capacities. They rule our thoughts, determining which shall appear and be strong and which shall pass from light into obscurity. . . .We may think of habits as means, waiting, like tools in a box, to be used by conscious resolve. But they are something more than that. They are active means, means that project themselves, energetic and dominating ways of acting.[11]

On the one hand, then, habit is the means by which immediate sensuous elements are enriched because the mind brings its previous experience to bear upon them in response. On the other hand, the body's tendencies to act, habits, are enriched insofar as the immediate sensuous elements are added as more signs for the body to act on these tendencies. However, if the mind had no way of picking out and weighing sensuous elements according to their degree of significance, it would be stuck in a perpetual cogwheel of association in which every felt detail would be connected to every other. The effect would be a rush of previous experience into the present without the ability to anticipate and direct future adjustments, leaving a jumbled and flat experience with no perspective. Therefore, the mind has a dissociating task that develops out of and accompanies its connecting, or associating, function. As Dewey suggests, dissociation is "giving some element in an association predominance over other," or the emphasis of some element and the neglect of others with reference to their value towards some end.[12] For example, after weeks of attempting to ride everything from surface chop to long-period ground swell, the surfer comes to associate the ground swell with a more controlled, smoother, and longer ride. Out of her previous associations, then, she begins to distinguish the difference in quality and value between the chop and the swell. Sitting atop her board facing out to sea, she looks past the thin, ill-formed chop to focus on a thick-bodied line of water that will serve her better in realizing the ideal of a good ride. Dissociation, then, allows the mind to select out of its external concerns those elements that bear some connection to the developing interests of the organism as a whole. Thus, according to Dewey, the apperceptive functions of association and dissociation cut the way for attention proper.

Attention is that activity of the self which connects all elements presented to it into one whole, with reference to their ideal significance; that is, with reference to the relation which they bear to some intellectual end. The essential characteristic of attention is, therefore, activity directed towards some end. Ultimately the end is the self. The various activities of attention are based in the interests of the self, and directed towards ends which will satisfy the self, by fulfilling these interests. Its process is such a direction of its own contents that these ends will be reached. Starting-point, goal, and way are all found in the self, therefore. Attention is thus a process of self-development.[13]

As Dewey suggests here, attention is both deliberate and future-oriented. It is the more assiduous and concentrated activity in apperception that selects and shapes sensuous material into a connection with some on-going interest or habit of the self. For example, the surfer comes to associate wind as an integral fact of her activity. At first, it may seem inconsequential, and then, perhaps, incessant and annoying, roughing up the sea, jostling her about, and disrupting her rhythm. At first, the wind simply is nothing more to her than one big nebulous irritant. Over time, though, the surfer sees that changes in particular qualities of the wind, such as its intensity and direction, have different effects on the sea that, in turn, affect the quality of her activity. On-shore winds can build up the surf but can blow so hard that the surf becomes too rough to ride; off-shore winds can clean up the break but also can be so brisk as to flatten it out. Therefore, the surfer develops an interest in weather patterns with particular reference to how their characteristic winds affect the surf. While weather forecasts once meant nothing to her, now the surfer attends to the forecasts, selecting out barometric pressure readings, pressure system movements, wind speed, direction, and period. She then compares the particular measurements of these selected out qualities with measurements she has experienced before. Through this comparison, she gains a more defined signal or idea of what the sea conditions will be like, when and where she should surf, and what equipment to take. Thus, her attention to weather has added further significance to her activity by defining the particulars that affect it, which enables her to gain more control over her movements in response. In this sense, as Dewey points out, attention is a process of self-development. It is the means by which the individual selects and adjusts stimuli with reference to some end or ideal of interest. Thus, retention and apperception constitute the fundamental processes out of which perception, memory, imagination, and thinking develop, all stages of knowledge, and knowledge is power.

STAGES OF KNOWLEDGE

As Dewey suggests, knowing is the self-adjusting process by which the mind reads significance into stimuli by connecting these with some end of interest.

> Adjustment is the process by which the self so connects itself with the presented datum that this becomes a sign, or symbolic –points to something beyond its own new existence, and hence has meaning. The fact known is not a bare fact, that is, an existence implying not constructive activity of intelligence, but is idealized fact, existence upon which the constructive intelligence has been at work. That which is not thus idealized by the mind has no existence for intelligence. All knowledge is thus, in a certain sense, self-knowledge. Knowing is not the process by which ready-made objects impress themselves upon the mind, but is the process by which self renders sensations significant by reading itself into them.[14]

Another way to put this is that "knowing" is a more general term for the underlying processes of retention and apperception that constitute intellectual life. "Knowledge," then, refers to the product of these processes, that is, to the meaning of stimuli crystallized at some point within the on-going circuit of activity towards some end. Therefore, perception, memory, imagination, and thinking are all points or stages within on-going activity in which the meaning of stimuli becomes clearer and richer. As Dewey suggests, these are stages of intelligence progressively realizing itself.[15] More specifically, perception is that stage in the activity of mind in which a stimulus is connected or associated with an on-going interest such that the stimulus comes to represent a definite object for a particular purpose. For example, a citrus farmer interested in maintaining a healthy grove sees small round holes in the leaves on several trees. Immediately, he connects these holes with similar ones that he has seen before gnawed by aphids. The farmer perceives these holes to be not only the work of aphids but as indicators of a possible infestation problem. Or, a sailor looks out over a smooth lake surface until her eyes come to rest upon a thick body of choppy whitecaps that extend beyond her eyesight. Fixing her sight on one spot amid the chop, she notices that the whitecaps move steadily from north to south. She, therefore, perceives this movement to be the evidence of a north wind gust, even though she has not yet felt the wind sweep across her skin, which would further confirm her perception. Now, according to Dewey, every perception depends upon memory in order to give sense and connection to the perceived elements with the rest of one's experience. That is, every perception involves the rushing forth of some past relation of the self such that the immediate stimulus gains a temporal and, therefore, continuous connection with one of the self's particular tendencies to act. Thus, the farmer perceives the holes in his citrus leaves to be the result of aphids because he recognizes the characteristics of these holes to be similar to ones that once called out a certain response from him with reference to these pests. Memory, then, is that point in apperception in which some particular characteristic of a present stimulus instantaneously is dissociated from the rest of its attendant qualities and is reconnected with a similar characteristic experienced in the past that has been retained as an idea. This reconnection is the work of imagination.

As Dewey defines it, imagination is "that operation of the intellect which embodies an idea in a particular form or image."[16] That is, as the prevailing quality calls out some idea or retained coordination to act, the mind mechanically associates other similar or congruent characteristics once experienced with the present quality. The effect, then, is a more or less vivid picture of an idea filled out with sensible details. For example, the sailor picks out the whitecaps moving from north to south and recognizes them to be similar to the effects of a north wind she has once experienced. These particular whitecaps may call up certain feelings associated with that experience: the chill of frothy air and the fresh smell of ocean, a brilliant white sail against a powder-blue sky, and curses of anxiety at the wind gusts. These curses of anxiety, in turn, may call up other experiences the sailor has had in which sailors scurried to adjust sails in order to maintain their course. Thus, the idea of sailing initially called up by the perception of the present whitecaps becomes filled in with particular qualities from past occasions that cohere into an image, or a more or less sensible presence. This is what Dewey refers to as "mechanical imagination" because it functions implicitly within the complete activity of apperception. However, when the mind focuses its activity upon the abstracted meaning or significance of some stimuli with the direct intention to supplement this idea with just those qualities that help sharpen its definition, then mechanical imagination shades off into creative imagination and thinking proper.[17]

As Dewey suggests about all of these stages of knowledge, the distinction between creative imagination and thinking is one of emphasis within the continuous circuit of intellectual life. "In imagination the emphasis is upon this particular form, while in thinking the particular form is neglected in behalf of the universal content."[18] That is, thinking refers to the grasping of and attending to the idea or meaning holding together the facts of experience. It consists of conception, judgment, and reasoning, all integral aspects of this one fluid activity. More specifically, conception is the isolating of and focusing in on some particular activity retained as a sensory-motor response by the individual that provides the basis for a definite and meaningful relation between the individual and stimuli. It is the coming to a sharper awareness of what one is about, of what one is doing.

Conception is the apperception of the apperceptive process. The self here makes its own idealizing, relating activity its object of knowledge; it grasps this activity, and the product is the concept. Conception is, in short, but the development of the idealizing activity involved in all knowledge to the point where it gains distinct conscious recognition, freed from its sensuous, particular detail.[19]

As Dewey points out, every mental state, from perception to reasoning, will call up some degree of sensuous detail cohering as an image or picture. When the surfer thinks about the activity of surfing, she imagines the essential elements of the planing activity in water and under some sort of weather conditions. However, the emphasis on detail is secondary to the way or method of activity. "The concept is the power, capacity, or function of the image or train of images to stand for some mode of mental action, and it is the mode of action which is general."[20] Thus, the surfer from the earlier example abstracts the concept of planing the water from the weather forecast, that is, she becomes aware of the fact that what gives this forecast particular meaning is its reference to the activity of surfing that she reads into it. Or, from serious meteorological study, she has gained an understanding of the evaporation-condensation cycle as well as the relationship between temperature, pressure, and wind speed, and has, thus, developed a concept of weather as an activity. Moreover, she has learned from repeated experience that weather as an activity has particular effects on her favorite surf break that are dependent upon variations in these weather elements. Therefore, she has made her concepts of weather and surfing more definite in meaning by realizing the relationship between these two activities.

After reviewing the particular characteristics of the weather forecast, and from memory of previous experiences in the water under similar weather conditions, the surfer develops an estimation embodied in an image of what the surf conditions will be like as this weather system unfolds. This estimating amounts to judging, or "the express reference of the idea or universal element to reality," the truth of which depends upon the degree of harmony between idea and the facts at hand.[21] In this particular example, the surfer's judgment is the affirmation that the particular characteristics of this weather activity should produce certain effects not only at her surf break but at all other surf breaks given similar geographic conditions. As the system pushes through, she goes out to check to see if her judgment about the forecast actually matches the sea conditions that she expected. Reasoning, then, as Dewey suggests, is the recognition of why there is agreement or disagreement between ideas and facts. It is "that act of mind which recognizes those relations of any content of consciousness through which it has the meaning which it has, or is what it is."[22] Thus, the surfer reasons or brings into focus the idea that the wave height has increased because of the increase in on-shore winds from a counter-clockwise rotation of air mass, which, in turn, is caused by falling atmospheric pressure. Or, she reasons that the wave height has not increased because the system stalled and thus the expected wind pattern favorable for building surf did not materialize. In either case, however, her reasoned understanding of the causal connection between weather and waves in general enables her better to anticipate the effects of this activity in these particular circumstances. As a result of this knowledge, she can call up a more precise image of herself surfing under these specific conditions and, thus, select the proper equipment with more accuracy. Furthermore, the accuracy of her judgment as to the proper means to the end of planing the water is worked out or realized throughout the activity. That is, her qualitative sense or feel about the degree of this harmony resonates back to her attention through her conduct and serves either to increase the significance and emotional trigger of this line of discharge or to indicate the need to modify it further in order to meet the circumstances. Either way, she gains a more sensitive, refined, and significant control of her particular activity. Put in broader terms, she gains more power to develop herself as one who not only engages in this type of activity but, by virtue of this line of conduct, develops another apperceptive means by which to widen and unify her other activities. Simply put, she increases her power of self-realization.

> We here reach an ultimate fact in the psychological constitution of man. He
> has the power of determining himself. He has the power of setting up an
> ideal of what he would have himself be, and this ideal in form depends only
> upon himself. . . .This ideal of self-realization depends for its form upon the
> self and upon that alone. For its content, for its specific and concrete filling
> up it depends, as previously shown, upon his education, surroundings, etc.[23]

SUMMARY: HABIT AS THE POWER TO ACT

In the quotation above, Dewey is suggestive of the thesis of this chapter. That is, according to Dewey's account, the human organism acquires all the powers of conscious activity necessary to define what it is about in the world and to adjust itself as the demands upon this activity changes. More specifically, this conscious activity consists of the apperceptive and retentive processes of the central nervous system. These complementary processes function to make up what Dewey calls the self-executing mechanism of habit. Put in psycho-physiological terms, habit amounts to the tendency or predisposition to conduct nervous energy along a previously formed sensory-motor channel. It is the means whereby the environment is taken into and becomes a part of the self, and by which the self affects and becomes a part of the environment. Furthermore, habit is the mainspring of intelligence, as Dewey would say. It is through the conduction of nervous energy along these formed sensory-motor channels that the organism's intellectual functions of ordering and attending develop. As Dewey puts it in *Human Nature and Conduct*, "Concrete habits do all the perceiving, recognizing, imagining, recalling, judging, conceiving and reasoning that is done. 'Consciousness,' whether as a stream or as special sensations and images, expresses functions of habits, phenomena of their formation, operation, their interruption and reorganization."[24] Thus, in form, habit enables individuals to determine themselves along a more or less definite line of activity.

Now, as indicated throughout this and the previous chapters, habit is acquired and developed in the individual through his or her constant interaction with a particular environment. Insofar as this environment always involves other human beings engaged in particular activities, then it is warranted to say that an individual's association and interaction with a particular social environment influences the development of his or her habits. That is, the social environment gives particular content and meaning to habit, as Dewey suggests above. To the extent that individuals react similarly to similar circumstances, then it may be said that habits of action are shared, communicated, and transmitted. Thus, habit is ineluctably social and may be referred to as social habit or practice. It is through particular social practices, therefore, that individuals gain not only shared means of affecting their environment but common standards by which to judge and guide their activities as they are directed towards particular shared ends or ideals. From the side of the self, social practices provide the individual with the means to develop particular motive, interest, and character through action. From the side of the social environment, social practices serve as the very foundation whereby associative and communal life are realized, widen, and expanded. Thus, it is through the judgments of effects within particular shared practices that the distinction between that which serves to expand the self and that which functions to narrow the self becomes clear. In other words, the discrimination between "power of" and "power over" self-realization always takes place within and with reference to the ideals and standards of particular shared practices. Therefore, in order to underscore the idea that this distinction has as much to do with particular social functions (and therefore community life) as it does with a particular self, it will be important to work out the nature of the ideal as it emerges from within social habit.

NOTES

[1] John Patrick Diggins, *The Promise of Pragmatism: Modernism and the Crisis of Knowledge and Authority* (Chicago: The University of Chicago Press, 1994). Diggins writes, "As a Darwinian naturalist, Dewey treats the human species as an 'organism,' and he confines his analysis to a biological vocabulary that need not probe the depths of motivation but instead focuses on struggle, adaptation, and survival. Dewey also assumes that the precarious status of existence is as progressive as it is provocative, for the instabilities of the environment give rise to intelligence as an instrument of control" (p. 287). In turn, according to Diggins, "Dewey not only refused to give much attention to power and its origins, he also had no idea where to look for it other than as some kind of aberration" (p. 288). See also pp. 280-321.

[2] C. Wright Mills, *Sociology and Pragmatism: The Higher Learning in America*, edited by Irving Louis Horowitz (New York: Paine-Whitman Publishers, 1964): p. 382.

[3] John Dewey, *Human Nature and Conduct: An Introduction to Social Psychology* (New York: Henry Holt and Company, 1922): pp. 14-15.

[4] John Dewey, *Psychology* (1887) *John Dewey, The Early Works, 1882-1898*, vol. 2, edited by Jo Ann Boydston (Carbondale: Southern Illinois University Press, 1967).

[5] Dewey, *Psychology, The Early Works*, vol. 2, p.78.

[6] Dewey, *Psychology, The Early Works*, vol. 2, p. 89.

[7] Dewey, *Psychology, The Early Works*, vol. 2, p. 85. As Dewey suggests, "The mind connects all sensations as far as possible into one total maximum experience. . . .The discovery of laws, the

classification of facts, the formation of a unified mental world, are all outgrowths of the mind's hunger for the fullest experience possible at the least cost" (p. 85).

[8] Dewey, *Psychology, The Early Works*, vol. 2, pp. 78-79.

[9] Dewey, *Psychology, The Early Works*, vol. 2, p. 93.

[10] Dewey, *Psychology, The Early Works*, vol. 2, pp. 100-102.

[11] Dewey, *Human Nature and Conduct*, p. 25. Dewey further writes, "The essence of habit is an acquired predisposition to ways or modes of response, not to particular acts except as, under special conditions, these express a way of behaving. Habit means special sensitiveness or accessibility to certain classes of stimuli, standing predilections and aversions, rather than bare recurrence of specific acts. It means will" (p. 42).

[12] Dewey, *Psychology, The Early Works*, vol. 2, p. 105.

[13] Dewey, *Psychology*, The Early Works, vol. 2, p. 118.

[14] Dewey, *Psychology, The Early Works*, vol. 2, pp. 125-126.

[15] Dewey, *Psychology, The Early Works*, vol. 2, pp. 137-213. As Dewey puts it, "We may say, therefore, that the development of knowledge is a process of increasing idealization from the less to the more significant. Since significance consists in relations, we may say that the growth of knowledge is measured by the extent of relations concerned. Each advancing stage is characterized by the development of a new and wider-reaching sphere of relations. These three modes of statement may be summed up by saying that intelligence is a process of realization of itself. . . .There will be, therefore, various stages in the process. . . .These are the so-called faculties of knowledge, which, therefore, are not various powers of the mind, but mark various stadia of its development" (pp.137-138).

[16] Dewey, *Psychology, The Early Works*, vol. 2, p. 168.

[17] Dewey, *Psychology, The Early Works*, vol. 2, pp. 168-175.

[18] Dewey, *Psychology, The Early Works*, vol. 2, p. 177. See also pp. 168-173 for the distinction that Dewey makes between these two stages.

[19] Dewey, *Psychology, The Early Works*, vol. 2, p. 180.

[20] Dewey, *Psychology, The Early Works*, vol. 2, p. 179.

[21] Dewey, *Psychology, The Early Works*, vol. 2, p. 186.

[22] Dewey, *Psychology, The Early Works*, vol. 2, pp. 192-193.

[23] Dewey, *Psychology, The Early Works*, vol. 2, p. 351.

[24] Dewey, *Human Nature and Conduct*, p. 177.

HABIT AS SOCIAL PRACTICE: A MEANS FOR JUDGING POWER

According to the previous chapters, the acquisition of habit is the means by which individuals gain a more sensitive and controlled interaction with their environment. By virtue of their activities, they come to widen and enhance the significance of their interests. In a word, habit means growth, the permanent end of which is a fuller expression of the self. The growth of the individual, however, can continue only by securing its proper conditions, which always includes attention to the specific needs, desires, expectations, and activities of other human beings. Since habit grows only through the individual's interaction with a social environment, he or she has an obligation to nourish those habits in others that lead each to a further realization of one's self and to a more enriched connection with each other. In other words, the ideal of self-growth consists in bringing about a more perfect unity between individual happiness and the happiness of others, the social welfare. Stated in this way, however, the ideal of self-growth remains abstract and vague. Therefore, working out the nature of the ideal of self-realization in this chapter will serve several functions.

First, it will help underscore the inherent connection between the individual and others as this connection evolves through shared activities aimed at bringing about shared ends. Second, working out the human being's inherent social nature will provide the foundation to establish the ideal of individual happiness and social welfare as a direct reflection of this nature in generic form, the particular content and meaning of which depends upon the range and depth of shared activities. It will help make the point, in other words, that the meaning of the ideal sprouts and grows organically from within particular shared activities. Third, the ideal serves as the criterion by which to make a distinction between right and wrong conduct. Furthermore, the ideal implies that judgments between power as enhancement and power as domination must be made on the basis of the same criterion as any judgment about conduct: according to the general ideal of individual happiness and social welfare defined in specific terms from within shared practices. Finally, working out the ideal of self-realization will serve as the necessary foundation in subsequent chapters to respond to Dewey's critics and to suggest how an understanding of Dewey's idea of power requalifies faith in a democratic experience.

THE SOCIAL INDIVIDUAL

Simply put, the human organism must digest, direct, and renew the forces of the environment that sustain it. To say that the life-sustaining activities of any one individual always imply some activity on the part of others is to suggest the commonplace idea that others are necessary nutrients in the environment. Their lives stimulate impulse and stoke emotion. Their occupations furnish purpose and sharpen skill. Their expressions conspire in memory, fuel imagination, and haunt plans. In other words, the joys and sufferings of others are metabolized into every fiber of the individual's conduct. As Dewey points out, the inherent social nature of the individual constitutes a fundamental fact of existence.

Since habits involve the support of environing conditions, a society, or some specific group of fellow-men, is always accessory before and after the fact. Some activity proceeds from a man; then it sets up reactions in the surroundings. Others approve, disapprove, protest, encourage, share and resist. Even letting a man alone is a definite response. Envy, admiration, and imitation are complicities. Neutrality is non-existent. Conduct is always shared; this is the difference between it and a physiological process. It is not an ethical "ought" that conduct should be shared. It is social, whether bad or good.[1]

Dewey's reminder here that conduct always is shared entails several important implications. Since the individual must continue enlisting the support of others for growth, he or she must develop some degree of interest in their modes of response and their expectations of the consequences as a result of these responses. That is, if he or she is to acquire the skills necessary to become a part of the group, he or she must assimilate not only its likes, dislikes, desires, purposes, and plans but also its demands that these plans be carried out in particular ways. As Dewey puts it,

A being whose activities are associated with others has a social environment. What he does and what he can do depend upon the expectations, demands, and condemnations of others. A being connected with other human beings cannot perform his own activities without taking the activities of others into account. For they are indispensable conditions of the realization of his tendencies. When he moves, he stirs them and reciprocally.[2]

This social nature implies that the individual's activity is the particular conduction of some specific social custom, habit, or practice. Shared practices provide the individual with particular goods to be realized. They supply specific ends, aims, and purposes by which to develop interest, desire, judgment, and motive. They stimulate, organize, and direct the individual's senses, attention, and motion. In effect, shared practices are organs of intelligence.[3]

At the same time, all shared practices take place in reference to particular circumstances, the demands and requirements of which serve as checks on the individual to guide and modify his or her action. The social consequences of the individual's action return back to his or her attention and, more or less, set up as expectations and standards inside him or her by which he or she develops a sense of responsibility, duty, and obligation. It is by means of social practices, then, that the individual develops a sense of right and wrong conduct in realizing the good. Dewey eloquently puts the significance of the return in this way:

The social environment may be as artificial as you please. But its action in response to ours is natural not artificial. In language and imagination we rehearse the responses of others just as we dramatically enact other consequences. We foreknow how others will act, and the foreknowledge is the beginning of judgment passed on action. We know with them; there is conscience. An assembly is formed within our breast which discusses and appraises proposed and performed acts. The community without becomes a forum and tribunal within, a judgment-seat of charges, assessments, and exculpations. Our thoughts of our own actions are saturated with the ideas that others entertain about them, ideas which have been expressed not only in explicit instruction but still more effectively in reaction to our acts.[4]

In short, social practices develop character, the pivot upon which desire and consequences, good and right are unified and interpenetrate each other in concrete deed. Through this concrete unification in deed, new ends, interests, and associations emerge as added values and resources. Along with the growth of interests, there is an increase in responsibilities and obligations, as well as the possibility that interests will conflict within individuals and between them too. The fact of conflict not only divides and disrupts activity but, paradoxically, imbues it with a suspense and indefiniteness that makes social change and growth possible. Thus, the individual acts in light of conflict so as to bring about a wider and more thorough unity between specific goods and standards inherent to some particular social practice. Through this effort, the act leads to a further search for those shared habits, those modes of social intelligence, that nourish a fuller expression through more diverse and sensitive fellowships with others. Or, the individual acts so as to ossify and stunt the expansion of shared goods and standards. In effect, he or she cuts off interest from a more flourishing connection with others. As Dewey suggests, social customs or practices serve as the means whereby the individual gives concrete detail and meaning to "individual happiness" and "social welfare."

We traverse a spiral in which social customs generate some consciousness of interdependencies, and this consciousness is embodied in acts which in improving the environment generate new perceptions of social ties, and so on forever. The relationships, the interactions are forever there as fact, but they acquire meaning only in the desires, judgments and purposes they awaken. . . .Morals is connected with actualities of existence, not with ideals, ends and obligations independent of concrete actualities. The facts upon which it depends are those which arise out of active connections of human beings with one another, the consequences of their mutually intertwined activities in the life of desire, belief, judgment, satisfaction and dissatisfaction. In this sense conduct and hence morals are social: they are not just things which ought to be social and which fail to come up to the scratch. But there are enormous differences of better and worse in the quality of what is social. Ideal morals begin with the perception of these differences.[5]

Emerging from within the activities of human kind, the ideal of self-realization serves as an absolute yet flexible foot-rule by which individuals guide themselves in their responsibilities to bring about a more sympathetic and intelligent development of both character and community. As a standard, the ideal suggests that the value of conduct must be judged according to the degree to which motive issues forth in deed to enhance the human capacities to continue searching and realizing the meaning of individual happiness in connection with the happiness of others. Therefore, since the ideal of self-realization is the crux of Dewey's conception of power, it is necessary to show how this ideal forms through the development of character.

CHARACTER AS THE WAY OF DEFINING AND MEASURING THE SELF

To Dewey, "character" simply refers to the way in which the individual coordinates or conducts him or herself. More specifically, character signifies the manner in which the individual directs and controls his or her various impulses into a more or less significant, unified end of response.[6] Dewey argued that judgments about the goodness and rightness of activity are simply phases within the expression of some character. That is, the goodness and rightness of activity are determined always on the basis of some character attempting to discover and judge the significance of what he or she is about in the world. From the psychological standpoint, this amounts to the individual's determination of the consequences of some conduct on the growth of his or her interests, skills, desires, attitudes, habits, and ways of forming ends. From the social point of view, it is the individual's appraisal of the specific conditions (the arrangements, opportunities, and materials) set up in consequence of some conduct as these influence the active participation and development of others. In essence, the ideal as both good and standard is all one with some character defining and measuring itself in the concrete terms of some particular activity. Working out the ideal as it grows out of character will suggest that judgments of power are themselves one with this defining and measuring.

The Development of Character by Means of Social Practice

According to Dewey, the human organism is, more or less, constant activity, or as he puts it, "one uninterrupted, continuous redistribution of mass in motion."[7] The last chapter suggested that this redistribution involves the apperceptive and retentive processes of the central nervous system. These two processes work together to form sensory-motor coordinations that enable the organism to respond to its environment. Once formed, all sensory-motor coordinations are retained as nervous channels by which the organism may regulate the conduction of its energy in the future. The tendency or predisposition to conduct nervous energy along previously formed channels is what Dewey calls impulse, the development of which he termed habit. According to Dewey, habit refers to the build-up of a well-defined, self-executing mode of activity through the frequent association of various impulses. It develops by hitting upon and securing a combination of impulses according to the degree of pleasure, control, and harmony in meeting the demands of circumstance. However, whether pleasurable or painful, harmonious or discordant, the effects of acting upon an impulse are returned and retained in association with the other impulses. This return constitutes the consequence and significance of a line of activity. Since the association of various impulses makes up habit, the expression of one impulse tends to stimulate other impulses, which, in turn, brings to attention the prevailing consequences associated with these impulses. These consequences modify the inducing impulse by signaling the effects to be had if the particular impulse is followed out. In this sense, the results of previous experience serve as the standard to measure the value of the impulse, thus reacting into it so as to inhibit, stimulate, or reinforce its further expression. Simply put, the consequences associated with past experience give relation and significance to the impulse calling them up. Dewey calls this back reference to consequences "the mediation of impulse" and argues, furthermore, that this mediation is "the psychological basis of moral conduct."[8]

> Psychologically, the mediation of impulse (a) idealizes the impulse, gives it its value, its significance or place in the whole system of action, and (b) controls, or directs it. The fundamental ethical categories result from this distinction. The worth of an impulse is, psychologically, the whole set of experiences which, presumably (that is, upon the best judgment available) it will call into being. This, ethically, constitutes the goodness (or badness) of the impulse –the satisfaction (or dissatisfaction) which it carries. But the thought of the consequences which will follow, their conscious return back into the impulse, modify it –check it, increase it, alter it. . . .In this modification, through reaction of anticipated experiences, we have the basis of what, ethically, we term obligation –the necessity of modifying any particular expression of impulse by the whole system of which it is one part.[9]

As indicated earlier, Dewey maintains that social practices are the means by which individuals develop character by forming ends and meeting expectations. Insofar as individuals are born into the particular attitudes and dispositions of their social environment, then, in a sense, character happens to them. A child born into an athletic family will have her tendencies of strength, agility, and speed aroused and directed according to the particular activities in which the family engages. If she grows up in a family of unicyclists, she will develop some degree of affection for and attention to the one-wheel frame and how to operate it. Through coaxing by the others and through her own trial and error, she forms an initial idea of unicycling as the ability to stay upright while pedaling forward. She comes to see that the front pedal pushes her weight backward; the back pedal throws her weight forward. Once she is able to pedal a few turns, she begins to see that pedaling fast requires more leg speed than strength but forces the wheel too far in front of her weight; pedaling slow requires more strength but drags the wheel behind her. Thus, she develops an interest in the skills necessary to conduct herself according to her idea. The interest refers to the coordination of her tendencies that give her a sense of pivoting balance and recovering counterbalance, the overall habit of which itself becomes an impulse urging forward like a craving to be satisfied. The child, therefore, attends to those objects and conditions that will afford her the opportunity to act upon this impulse whenever possible. Dewey calls the satisfaction or expression of an immediate impulse its natural good. However, as Dewey points out, one tendency is never isolated from the others that make up the individual but gets its meaning and direction from the other impulses that it calls up.

If, for example, every time the child becomes easily frustrated and angered in her attempt to ride her unicycle, her siblings may mock her attitude so as to suggest that crybabies will not be tolerated. Her parents may underscore the need to modify her frustration by taking whatever measures necessary to make the point that the activity demands perseverance, attention, and toughness instead of anger and puniness. Or, if the family unicycles along their neighborhood street, the bare impulse to ride the unicycle must be mediated by other factors. A neighbor's trampled azalea bush as a result of the child's inattention to her surroundings may cause her to be the object of the neighbor's scorn. Indifference to oncoming cars while riding in the street may have endangering results not only for the child and her playmates but also for the motorists and neighbors as well. In a sense, her indifference bites back at her. She gets hurt or her parents scold her for acting carelessly. To the degree that the child is forced to attend to the consequences of her actions, then, these consequences return back into her original impulse and become a constituent, living part of it. The exhilarating, the sharing, the mocking, the scorning, and the scolding give concrete relation and significance to the impulse. From now on, they serve as the basis by which to check, measure, and modify the impulse. As Dewey suggests, the returned consequences are the law of the impulse. "They determine in what form, under what conditions of time, place, and quality, it may be satisfied. Thus they determine or measure its value; they say to it: You are not what you are alone or in yourself, but your value is what it is in relation to us. In this aspect, the induced experiences (reason, for short) are the standard of measurement for the natural impulse."[10]

According to Dewey, the suffering of consequences works back into the impulse to change its natural good into a mediated or moral good. That is, as returned effects, their qualities are felt in association with the impulse and set up into the fiber of its idea. To the degree that the consequences involve others, their return gives the impulse a social relation and definition. Now it is in this sense that an assembly or tribunal of others forms within the individual. Every time the individual's attention hits upon the idea, the social consequences emerge as anticipated outcomes. Insofar as they are felt effects to be avoided or produced, the consequences of an idea are equivalent to demands for certain ways of behaving. Their authority rests in the degree of promise for pleasure, pain, help, protest, and support in reference to some line of activity. They oblige the individual to measure his or her activity accordingly. As Dewey points out, the basis by which the individual weighs the value of his or her impulse in reference to social claims "is found in the fact that some acts tend to narrow the self, to introduce friction into it, to weaken its power, and in various ways to disintegrate it, while other acts tend to expand, invigorate, harmonize, and in general organize the self."[11]

For example, the child's refusal to consider her siblings' demands that she control her anger brings about her isolation from them. In turn, her anger diminishes her opportunities to ride the unicycle with them and to learn new skills and abilities from them. The child's acts of anger, therefore, have weakened her ability to refine her strength, agility, and speed and to expand this interest through other related activities. In short, her anger diminishes her power. It prevents her from finding her control through an activity that otherwise defines her. If, however, the child tempers her anger into a determined focus by the idea of her isolation, she may continue to develop the athletic skills necessary to make her balance more sensitive and stable. Or, if she converts her inattention to traffic into an alertness for others by the thought of pain and disappointment, she will have gained further control of herself by learning to organize and adjust her impulses according to what they signify for her. She learns that being an alert steward of the road wins her parents' trust. The trust gained through unicycling may develop into a trust to use the kitchen stove by herself or to baby-sit her younger siblings. Now the child not only has organized and strengthened her power but has extended it as well. She has expanded her opportunities to draw on others as resources and to employ her developing judgment through associated activities that require more of her. In essence, she has changed the natural good of an impulse to harmonize with the social claims made upon it. As Dewey would say, she has mediated the good by the right and, thus, has expanded her idea of the ends, means, and responsibilities inherently necessary in satisfying her impulse.

> Others do not leave us alone. They actively express their estimates of good in demands made upon us. They accompany them with virtual promise of aid and support if their expectations are met, and with virtual threats of withdrawal of help, and of positive infliction of penalty, if we do not then take them into account in forming the purposes which control our own conduct. . . .When considered as claims and expectations, they constitute the Right in distinction from the Good. But their ultimate function and effect is to lead the individual to broaden his conception of the Good; they operate to induce the individual to feel that nothing is good for himself which is not also a good for others. They are stimuli to a widening of the area of consequences to be taken into account in forming ends and deducing what is Good.[12]

The good alloyed now with the right frames up the moral ideal. The degree of harmony forged between the individual's tendencies and their intrinsic social claims measures the degree of mediated satisfaction or happiness of the individual.[13] Insofar as the individual consciously tends toward this harmony in his or her activities, then the ideal as the good means the continued growth of happiness through the particular activities that define him or her. Since others are a part of the individual's tendencies, then, in broader terms, the ideal as the standard refers to the extent to which the individual's realization of his or her own happiness conduces to the happiness of others. As Dewey puts it, "The criterion thus comes to be only the generalized ideal, while the ideal is a specific definition of the more general standard. They are related as a foot-rule in the abstract, and this rule translated into the defined length of some portion of space. . . .If we look at this whole activity as that which the agent is urging towards in every act, it is Ideal; if we look at it as really deciding the nature and value of the act, it is Criterion."[14]

For instance, the girl realizes the good of her impulse to balance by being tenacious, watchful, and commanding in the circumstances through which she acts. Insofar as unicycling leads to other activities of interest (cooking and babysitting), the qualities inherent in the execution of these activities are associated with and signify each other. As practices, they call up each other, embodying each other, strengthening their unity and making their association more sensitive. Supported now by the trust built through unicycling, the girl rides the one-wheel miles away to baby-sit. The good of her original impulse has grown to include activities that entail additional capacities and special demands. Not only do the social demands multiply on her activity but apply across a wider context. On the one hand, the criterion by which the girl measures her behavior is the degree to which any one act strengthens or weakens the unity of her other tendencies, that is, the degree of happiness brought about after the fact of an act. On the other hand, the criterion (happiness as a standard of judgment) forces her to consider the particular social claims on her behavior beforehand and, therefore, guides her in forming a broader and more thorough idea of the good of her activity.

The Expression of Character and The Growth of Social Practice

As Dewey maintains, the forming and judging of ends and goods according to their moral significance is the application of character. Again, character refers to the way and extent in which the individual mediates his or her impulses, considers the demands on his or her behavior, sizes up the consequences and means of action, and determines the more satisfactory course to take. In essence, the expression of character amounts to growth in one way or another, not only for the individual but also for the community of associates whose demands are metabolized into the standard guiding his or her activity. According to Dewey, "Differences of moral value depend simply upon the range and thoroughness of this mediation –the completeness with which the consequences of an act are returned into the structure of the natural impulse."[15] Therefore, the determination of power as enhancement or domination is realized, more or less, through some character defining and measuring the moral significance of his or her activity. In order to work out this latter idea, it only is necessary to expand upon the example of the unicyclist who now has matured into a student of teaching.

Over time and through various activities associated with unicycling, the woman has developed particular powers of balance, agility, strength, conscientiousness, leadership, reflection, and investigation. Constant encouragement from others has led her to see that in order to improve and expand her abilities, she always must try to do the best that she can with the circumstances at hand. She realizes that doing the best she can requires thoughtful sensitivity to the social environment through which she acts. Therefore, the woman develops a concept of growth as the attending to, learning about, and enhancing the meaning of what she is about when she acts.

The woman now qualifies, guides, and measures her various activities according to her conception of growth such that learning itself urges forth as a habit to be satisfied. The habit of learning nourishes and strengthens her various tendencies with new details and resources. It becomes the prevailing quality unifying all of her conduct. It develops into such a dominant characteristic of the woman's activity that, when coupled with her more social impulses, she begins to see that it is her responsibility to instruct others to recognize the significance of learning for the development of their own activities. Thus, in a sense, the original activity of unicycling has led the woman to the practice of teaching.

Through study and trial, the woman begins to form a definite ideal of teaching. She realizes that good teaching aims to provide the experiences necessary to direct others to sense, test, measure, reflect upon, and develop an idea of what they are engaged in on their own. In short, she starts to see that good teaching cultivates the intellectual powers of attention, perception, memory, imagination, and conception in individuals such that they widen and deepen the significance of their own interests. However, in her attempt to bring about this good, she comes to understand that not all students are equally amenable to her instruction. Circumstances outside of and within her classroom distract students from attending to their interest, discouraging thought about particulars and encouraging either unreasoned conformity or blind rebellion to routine. Moreover, she senses among certain students an increasing lack of self-confidence to approach new situations and to use their intellectual powers to resolve challenging problems. This lack of self-confidence, in turn, reinforces debilitating impulses and creates a distaste for learning. In light of these insights, the teacher works to study and identify the particular circumstances that stunt her students' growth. She understands that she must become more flexible in her modes of instruction and more focused upon using these debilitating circumstances in ways that will stimulate interest, thought, and desire in her students. Therefore, the woman expands her idea of good teaching by noting further work to be done and taking the responsibility to engage in this work as the rightful means of achieving the good.

The fact that the woman has enhanced the good of teaching by refining her activities to meet further responsibilities does not mean that she will satisfy her obligations thoroughly enough every time. Furthermore, what she takes to be her teaching responsibilities in general may conflict with other responsibilities also called up to her attention under specific circumstances. Insofar as lapses and inconsistencies of responsibility return back to disrupt activity, then, the resulting conflict serves as a necessary flashpoint for moral struggle. That is, the individual finds herself at the center of competing impulses whose respective fulfillment lead her in separate directions, requiring opposing duties and dispositions from her. She feels herself divided, disorganized, confused, and troubled in her powers of activity. As Dewey suggests, "Only a signal flag of distress recalls consciousness to the task of carrying on."[16]

Although conflict serves as, what Dewey calls, a "sine qua non" of reflective thought, conflict by itself is not a sufficient factor to provoke the intellectual powers to their task. Depending upon the strength of interest and the steadfastness of character, the individual more or less either succumbs to the confusion because she cannot regain a clear idea of what she is about or perceives enough significance amid the confusion so as to set her attention to work. If the former be the case, then her particular powers of activity dry up; if the latter, then the conflict provides a forced opportunity for her to regain control and expand her idea of the good to be served. Something strikes an impulse in her that suggests other related impulses that work together as a whole activity. She senses the good of the activity and it surges forward as a desire. Remembering previous satisfactions of the activity, she imagines its execution in light of her present circumstances, paying particular attention to those factors that run counter to its fulfillment. Through the search, she focuses on some element that strikes an opposing impulse in her and that suggests its own supporting train of impulses. The individual starts to see her trouble now as a conflict of desires, of ends and goods whose competing ideas for action have to be reasoned through, broken down and recombined in imagination, weighed, and compared. As Dewey suggests, only creative imagination guided by acute conception and judgment can discover a broader significance for action and, thus, help re-establish a new equilibrium to character.[17]

> The poignancy of situations that evoke reflection lies in the fact that we really do not know the meaning of the tendencies that are pressing for action. We have to search, to experiment. Deliberation is a work of discovery. Conflict is acute; one impulse carries us one way into one situation, and another impulse takes us another way to a radically different objective result. Deliberation is not an attempt to do away with this opposition of quality by reducing it to one of amount. It is an attempt to uncover the conflict in its full scope and bearing. What we want to find out is what difference each impulse and habit imports, to reveal qualitative incompatibilities by detecting the different courses to which they commit us, the different dispositions they form and foster, the different situations into which they plunge us. . . .In short, the thing actually at stake in any serious deliberation is. . .what kind of person one is to become, what sort of self is in the making, what kind of world is in the making.[18]

As Dewey indicates, the conflict of desires entails several important implications for the judgment and direction of what kind of person one is to become. First, if the individual is to act at all, she must choose between competing impulses that involve sets of consequences that are entirely different from each other. That is, she must choose between modes of activity that will shape her character in different ways, or, at least, choose to modify the activities so as to strike a more comprehensive aim that will serve them all. Either way, choice entails growth of character in one direction or another. Furthermore, choice implies that the individual sees herself as the locus of control over her actions. Second, choice, in turn, involves the defining and measuring of character. It suggests that the individual, more or less, has the power to mediate her conflicting impulses, to reason through what effects each impulse will have on her habits as well as the habits of others, and to form an idea of an end that is the better for recovering a sense of meaningful action. Insofar as choice means settling upon an end to be served, then the individual regains specific motive force, or interest, to bring the end about in deed. Thus, prior to the act, the individual measures the range and thoroughness of habit that a deed will bring about, both for herself and for others. In essence, she judges the power of an act as either enhancing or debilitating to the overall good for individuals to direct the growth of their own conduct. Thus, her estimate of moral value amounts to an estimate of power relations based upon her notion of the good to be served and the right and wrong ways to serve it. However, the defining and measuring of character is not yet complete.

Through the execution of the act, the consequences return to fill out the significance of the individual's conduct and character. Dewey suggests that "prior to the act, the agent measures by his existing standard of good, and does the deed as good; afterward, the deed, in its full content, reveals his own character, and thus measures the standard."[19] That is, as the consequences return, the individual checks to see if her action adequately meets the demands and claims of right on her. In this sense, the standard (character) measures the act. To the extent that the act misses its mark, then it recoils with consequences, demands, and expectations not thought of beforehand. In this sense, the act tests the standard, notes deficiencies of character in forming and executing ends, and, therefore, reveals further work to be done.

To follow up on the example, the teacher encounters a group of youths who see her riding the unicycle along her neighborhood street. Their crude mode of inquiry into the activity reminds the teacher of the helpless yet rebellious attitudes of some students whom she had taught in the past. Sensing that the youths would benefit from the discipline and focus required by the activity, the teacher painstakingly explains unicycling in minute detail and encourages each youth to take a turn. While she focuses her attention on helping one, she notices that the others are smacking the branches of her neighbor's orange tree in a ravenous attempt to dislodge the fruit. The juicy oranges at the top of the tree stimulate the teacher's own desire to pick the fruit. Remembering past pleasures of eating oranges herself, she sympathizes with the youths' seemingly uncontrollable desire to get at their target. She also recognizes that they are damaging and taking from her neighbor's tree, which strikes a long established impulse in her that obliges her to stop them. However, she senses that even the mildest reprimand could damage her developing rapport with the youths and would detract from her power to teach them the goods of unicycling. Although she feels a conflict of desires, she vaguely recognizes her trouble as such. She chooses to continue instructing one youth as if oblivious to the activity of the others. When the rapacious youths have completed their pillaging, and without the simplest sign of gratitude, they abandon the teacher along with the sucked-clean orange carcasses scattered about the street.

As she picks up the discarded orange shells, the teacher realizes her deficiency in judging the moral value of the situation. The tattered fruit tree signals her shameful failure as a dutiful neighbor, and each orange peel serves as a mocking symbol that her ideal of good teaching was not encompassing enough. She judges that she failed to mediate her impulses properly such that teaching the youths a sense of conscientiousness for others emerged as a necessary part of her instructional and neighborly duties. Subsequently, she sees that her power both as a neighbor and as a teacher is diminished. Furthermore, she reasons that her failure to hold the youths to the task of considering others will perpetuate the dominion of their careless tendencies over both their characters and the social environment in which they act. The youths' inability to consider the demands of their social setting reduces their capacity to use others as resources and guides. In turn, their inconsiderateness not only cripples their control over their own growth by limiting their possibilities for developing insight and choice but sets up deleterious social arrangements in consequence. To the degree that the teacher metabolizes the new demands into the living structure of her action, she, therefore, enlarges her idea of the good guiding both her character and the community of others who have a share in her conduct. As Dewey puts it,

> Morals means growth of conduct in meaning; at least it means that kind of expansion in meaning which is consequent upon observations of the conditions and outcome of conduct. It is all one with growing. Growing and growth are the same fact expanded in actuality or telescoped in thought. In the largest sense of the word, morals is education. It is learning the meaning of what we are about and employing that meaning in action. The good, satisfaction, or "end," of growth of present action in shades and scope of meaning is the only good within our control, and the only one, accordingly, for which responsibility exits.[20]

THE IDEAL OF SELF-REALIZATION AS THE BASIS FOR JUDGING RELATIONS OF POWER

Up to this point, the study suggests that Dewey's idea of power is embedded deeply within his understanding of the ideal of self-realization. The previous chapter (Chapter Four) indicated that the apperceptive and retentive capacities of the central nervous system give the individual the power to conduct him or herself in the first place. These nervous processes enable the individual to form sensory-motor channels (habits), the continued development of which yields an expanding control, refinement, and significance for the individual's conduct. In the most general sense, Dewey's idea of power refers to the individual's ability to conduct him or herself through the acquisition of habit.

The present chapter expands upon the physio-psychological basis of habit by underscoring its inherent social nature. According to Dewey, it is a fundamental fact of existence that individuals operate through an environment that always involves others. In order for their habits to grow and flourish, they must be increasingly sensitive to, receptive and considerate of the needs, demands, and expectations of the social environment. Simply put, the individual's habits develop always in reference to the demands of others who share in the consequences of his or her conduct.

Social demands give point and direction to particular modes of activity. They require that the individual not only act to satisfy personal desires but act in such a way so as to satisfy and harmonize with the desires of others. Therefore, social practices provide the individual with an ideal that serves as both good and standard by which to judge the growth of individual interests. As pointed out earlier, the good of an activity amounts to the specific satisfactions that individuals intend to bring about through their particular powers of conduct. The standard refers to the degree of happiness actually brought about such that the individual's powers of control are extended and the social conditions are enriched. Thus, the individual defines and measures the moral significance of action according to the degree of overall happiness that it will produce. That is, the estimate of the significance of an act amounts to a judgment of the consequences as either enhancing or debilitating. Since individuals always act and judge with reference to a social environment, they are always in relations of power, insofar as power refers to the ability to act so as to have some degree of effect on the social environment. Therefore, individuals determine the significance of particular power relations by judging the effects of these relations on the growth of their own happiness in relation to that of others. Now, since differences in moral value depend upon the range and thoroughness of the individual's judgment of the consequences of action, differences in the identification and measurement of power relations also depend upon his or her judgment. This is not to suggest that individuals will judge the value of power rightly every time or that they will not experience a conflict of values within themselves or with others. As Dewey maintains, conflict should be expected as a prime opportunity for reflection about matters of power. To Dewey, some degree of judgment concerning the value of power is central to defining and measuring the proper conditions for further human growth.

The recognition that good is always found in a present growth of significance in activity protects us from thinking that welfare consists in a soup-kitchen happiness, in pleasures we can confer upon others from without. It shows that good is the same in quality wherever it is found, whether in some other self or in one's own. . . .To say that the welfare of others, like our own, consists in a widening and deepening of the perceptions that give activity its meaning, in an educative growth, is to set forth a proposition of political import. To "make others happy" except through liberating their powers and engaging them in activities that enlarge the meaning of life is to harm them and to indulge ourselves under the cover of exercising a special virtue. Our moral measure for estimating any existing arrangement or any proposed reform is its effect upon impulse and habit. Does it liberate or suppress, ossify or render flexible, divide or unify interest? Is memory made more apt and extensive or narrow and diffusively irrelevant? Is imagination diverted to fantasy and compensatory dreams, or does it add fertility to life? . . .To foster conditions that widen the horizons of others and give them command of their own powers, so that they can find their own happiness in their own fashion, is the way of social action.[21]

THE IDEAL OF SELF-REALIZATION AS THE DEMOCRATIC IDEAL

The significance of shared habit as the basis of Dewey's ideas of self-realization and, thus, democracy cannot be overstated. Fundamentally, shared habit is the source for self-realization. It forms the central nerve whereby the individual not only develops specific tendencies to act but more or less realizes his or her inherent connection to others as an indispensable condition for nourishing scattered impulses into serviceable capacities. To Dewey, habit does not refer simply to the mechanical ability to repeat acts. Habit more broadly serves as the medium by which people filter the special demands of others on their activity and refine their abilities in light of these demands. That is, shared habits direct attention, provoke thought, and incite emotion necessary for personal and social growth. Others command the individual to consider the significance of his or her actions more carefully. As claims of right, their expectations sharpen judgment about the direction and control over specific desires and inspire and enlarge the individual's idea of the good to be served. This is to say that, shared habits provide the individual with an intrinsic ideal for conduct that serves as both a good and standard. As the good or aim of conduct, the ideal refers to the individual's conscious tendency to develop particular capacities in harmony with the demands and needs of others as they develop their own powers. As the standard of judgment, the ideal refers to the degree to which the individual actually brings about this harmony in consequence of acting upon his or her conception of good. Through their attempts to realize a common good, individuals come to identify new interests and capacities for further growth, as well as additional responsibilities intrinsic to these new potentials. Thus, the ideal of self-realization entails two principles whose just relation makes up the democratic ideal: individual liberty and social equality.

> Liberty is that secure release and fulfillment of personal potentialities which take place only in rich and manifold association with others: the power to be an individualized self making a distinctive contribution and enjoying in its own way the fruits of association. Equality denotes the unhampered share which each individual member of the community has in the consequences of associated action. It is equitable because it is measured only by need and capacity to utilize, not by extraneous factors which deprive one in order that another may take and have.[22]

As pointed out earlier in this chapter, the growth of an individual's interests (personal liberty) takes place within and by virtue of a social environment. Those affected make claims upon the individual to act in such a way that is considerate of and fair to the full development of others (social equality). Justice, then, refers to the degree of harmony brought about in consequence of an individual's growth in relation to the special demands of others. To the extent that the phrase "the common good" refers to and is a measure of this harmony, then "the common good" also signifies a measure of justice at any one given time. As a measure of justice, the common good serves as a guide for considering broader social claims to fairness and thus for forming a more thorough idea of the social ends to be served.

> The tenor of this discussion is that the conception of common good, of general well-being, is a criterion which demands the full development of individuals in their distinctive individuality, not a sacrifice of them to some alleged vague larger good under the plea that it is "social." Only when individuals have initiative, independence of judgment, flexibility, fullness of experience, can they act so as to enrich the lives of others and only in this way can a truly common welfare be built up. The other side of this statement, and of the moral criterion, is that individuals are free to develop, to contribute and to share, only as social conditions break down walls of privilege and of monopolistic possession. . . .The criterion is identical in its political aspect with the democratic ideal. For democracy signifies, on one side, that every individual is to share in the duties and rights belonging to control of social affairs, and, on the other side, that social arrangements are to eliminate those external arrangements of status, birth, wealth, sex, etc., which restrict the opportunity of each individual for full development of himself. On the social side, it demands cooperation in place of coercion, voluntary sharing in a process of mutual give and take, instead of authority imposed from above. As an ideal of social life in its political phase it is much wider than any form of government, although it includes government in its scope. As an ideal, it expresses the need for progress beyond anything yet attained; for nowhere in the world are there institutions which in fact operate equally to secure the full development of each individual, and assure to all individuals a share in both the values they contribute and those they receive. Yet it is not "ideal" in the sense of being visionary and utopian; for it simply projects to their logical and practical limit forces inherent in human nature and already embodied to some extent in human nature. It serves accordingly as basis for criticism of institutions as they exist and of plans of betterment. . . . .Most criticisms of it are in fact criticisms of the imperfect realization it has so far achieved.[23]

Dewey's idea of democracy issues forth several important implications for social and political action. A just relation between liberty and equality can be built up, refined, and extended only according to the degree of cooperation between individuals in their various associations with each other. The activity of groups, then, must be directed toward expanding and enhancing the meaning of individual powers in such a way that others, both within and between groups, share in this meaning more equally and fully. Since groups are composed of individuals, each has a civic responsibility to form and nourish the conditions necessary for individual and social growth.[24] In this sense, the democratic ideal serves as both aim and standard guiding social action. Furthermore, a democratic ideal demands a democratic means for fulfillment. If individuals are to increase the shared fund of meaning by developing their particular capacities, they must become increasingly perceptive and sympathetic to the needs expressed in the growth of others. That is, they must have a developing awareness and concern for the actual and potential consequences of their actions. However, no one individual can fathom every possible effect of his or her actions. They require the responsive help from others to inform them of their efforts, to help them identify their incipient abilities, and to suggest contacts that might serve as resources for further growth. The voices of others more or less steer the individual to new social demands to which he or she should hold him or herself accountable. Therefore, the democratic ideal demands a constant communication between individuals that serves as a social radar.

According to Dewey, democracy necessitates a free and open exchange of perspectives about the consequences of conjoint action on the growth of habit, interest, and desire. Constant questioning and inquiry helps detect social inequalities that stunt individuals' growth and brings debilitating social arrangements to the light of discussion. However, Dewey had no illusion that unflagging watchfulness and discussion necessarily would bring about a greater democracy in practice. He clearly understood that individuals might not always perceive the consequences of social arrangements accurately or with greater insight—if they perceived them at all. He also acknowledged the existence of social forces insidiously designed not only to hinder the public's ability to detect harm but to enlist its deepest, most unquestioned sentiments in manufacturing private gain.[25] However, Dewey always maintained that perception and communication of some sort is a necessary condition for individuals to gather to deliberate about the significance and control of social consequences. "There can be no public without full publicity in respect to all consequences which concern it. Whatever obstructs and restricts publicity, limits and distorts public opinion and checks and distorts thinking on social action."[26] This is not to say, however, that the free exchange and discussion of ideas automatically leads to increased unity of interest. Discussion might illuminate a greater divergence of interests and therefore sharpen the lines of conflict. But, as Dewey suggests, "The method of democracy—insofar as it is that of organized intelligence—is to bring these conflicts out into the open where their special claims can be seen and appraised, where they can be discussed and judged in light of more inclusive interests than are represented by either of them separately."[27] In effect, the mutual give and take of discussion and persuasion conducted in good faith allows for a more informed intelligence than any one individual is capable of alone. The free and open exchange of ideas multiplies the possible range and thoroughness of perspective, which increases the likelihood of a more enlightened judgment and organization of conduct.

> Liberty to think, inquire, discuss, is central in the whole group of rights which are secured in theory to individuals in a democratic social organization. It is central because the essence of the democratic principle is appeal to voluntary disposition instead of to force, to persuasion instead of

coercion. Ultimate authority is to reside in the needs and aims of individuals as these are enlightened by a circulation of knowledge, which in turn is to be achieved by free communication, conference, discussion. Exchange of ideas, distribution of knowledge, implies a previous possession of ideas and information which is dependent upon freedom of investigation. Free circulation of intelligence is not enough barely of itself to effect the success of democratic institutions. But apart from it there is no opportunity either for the formation of a common judgment and purpose or for the voluntary participation of individuals in the affairs of government. For the only alternative to control by thought and conviction is control by externally applied force, or at best by unquestioned custom. Even the ballot, as the alternative to the bullet, has its ultimate value as a form of articulate expression of need and intention. The opportunity to communicate desire in this way is of value ultimately because it is a stimulus to the formation of informed judgment.[28]

Dewey's critics, however, suggest that his philosophical assumptions impair his method for identifying and resolving social conflict effectively. They claim that in effect of his philosophical stance, Dewey was unable to understand how individuals employ reason as a means to manipulate others subtlety into serving hidden selfish ends. In turn, his critics say, Dewey's appeal to conference and intelligence as the means to secure a greater social justice and liberty is meaningless at best and complicit in the manipulation of others by powerful self-interests at worst. Therefore, in order to judge the merits of these critics' claims, it is necessary to work out their various arguments in more detail.

NOTES

[1] John Dewey, *Human Nature and Conduct: An Introduction to Social Psychology* (New York: Henry Holt and Company, 1922): p. 16.

[2] John Dewey, *Democracy and Education: An Introduction to The Philosophy of Education* (New York: The Macmillan Company, 1916/1950): p. 14.

[3] In *Democracy and Education* Dewey writes, "In accord with the interests and occupations of the group, certain things become objects of high esteem; others of aversion. Association does not create impulses of affection and dislike, but it furnishes the objects to which they attach themselves. The way our group or class does things tends to determine the proper objects of attention, and thus to prescribe the directions and limits of observation and memory" (p. 20).

[4] Dewey, *Human Nature and Conduct*, p. 315.

[5] Dewey, *Human Nature and Conduct*, pp. 328-329.

[6] Dewey suggests that "we say character when we are thinking of the mediated impulses as the source from which all particular acts issue. . . .It designates the way in which impulses (varying, or course, in every person) are directed and controlled – that is, mediated. . . .Character includes the style and nature of the ends, the objects by which the individual mediates his impulses, and thus affords sufficient basis for taking into account the objective results of acts. . . .In a word, character is the unity, the spirit, the idea of conduct, while conduct is the reality, the realized or objective expression of character" [John Dewey, *The Study of Ethics: A Syllabus*, (1894), *John Dewey, The Early Works, 1882-1898*, vol. 4, edited by Jo Ann Boydston (Carbondale: Southern Illinois University Press, 1971): pp. 241-242].

[7] John Dewey, "The Reflex Arc Concept in Psychology," *John Dewey, The Early Works, 1882-1898*, vol. 5, edited by Jo Ann Boydston (Carbondale: Southern Illinois University Press, 1972): p. 103.

[8] Dewey, *The Study of Ethics: A Syllabus, The Early Works*, vol. 4, p. 236. As Dewey puts it, "Each impulse in its expression tends to call up other impulses; and it brings into consciousness other experiences. . . .In other words, the expression of every impulse stimulates other experiences and these react into the original impulse and modify it. This reaction of the induced experiences into the inducing impulse is the psychological basis of moral conduct."

[9] Dewey, *The Study of Ethics: A Syllabus, The Early Works*, vol. 4, pp. 238-239.

[10] Dewey, *The Study of Ethics: A Syllabus, The Early Works*, vol. 4, p. 248.

[11] Dewey, *The Study of Ethics: A Syllabus, The Early Works*, vol. 4, p. 244.

[12] John Dewey, *Ethics*, (1908/1932), *John Dewey, The Later Works, 1925-1953*, vol. 7, edited by Jo Ann Boydston (Carbondale: Southern Illinois University Press, 1985): pp. 224-225.

[13] In the *Ethics* Dewey writes, "Harmony as distinct from pleasure is a condition of the self. . . .A criterion can be given for marking off mere transient gratification from true happiness. The latter issues from objects which are enjoyable in themselves but which also reenforce and enlarge the other desires and tendencies which are sources of happiness. . . .Harmony and readiness to expand into union with other values is a mark of happiness. Isolation and liability to conflict and interference are marks of those states which are exhausted in being pleasurable" (p. 199).

[14] Dewey *The Study of Ethics: A Syllabus, The Early Works*, vol. 4, p. 288.

[15] Dewey, *The Study of Ethics: A Syllabus, The Early Works*, vol. 4, p. 238.

[16] Dewey, *Human Nature and Conduct*, p. 173. Dewey points out that "conflict is the gadfly of thought. It stirs us to observation and memory. It instigates to invention. It shocks us out of sheep-like passivity, and sets us at noting and contriving. Not that it always effects this result; but that conflict is a sine qua non of reflection and ingenuity" (p. 300).

[17] In *Human Nature and Conduct* Dewey suggests that "the release of some portion of the stock of impulses is an opportunity, not an end. In its origin it is the product of chance; but it affords imagination and invention their chance. The moral correlate of liberated impulse is not immediate activity, but reflection upon the way in which to use impulse to renew disposition and reorganize habit. . . .Impulse is needed to arouse thought, incite reflection and enliven belief. But only thought notes obstructions, invents tools, conceives aims, directs technique, and thus converts impulse into an art which lives in objects. Thought is born as the twin of impulse in every moment of impeded habit" (pp. 170-171).

[18] Dewey, *Human Nature and Conduct*, p. 216.

[19] Dewey, *The Study of Ethics: A Syllabus, The Early Works*, vol. 4, p. 297.

[20] Dewey, *Human Nature and Conduct*, p. 280.

[21] Dewey, *Human Nature and Conduct*, pp. 293-294.

[22] John Dewey, *The Public and Its Problems*, (Chicago: the Swallow Press Inc., 1927/1954): p.150.

[23] Dewey, *Ethics, The Later Works*, vol. 7, pp. 348-349.

[24] In *The Public and Its Problems*, Dewey provides a sense of the rights and responsibilities of democratic citizenship. "From the standpoint of the individual, it consists in having a responsible share according to capacity in forming and directing the activities of the groups to which one belongs and in participating according to need in the values which the groups sustain. From the standpoint of the groups, it demands liberation of the potentialities of members of a group in harmony with the interests and goods which are common. Since every individual is a member of many groups, this specification cannot be fulfilled except when different groups interact flexibly and fully in connection with other groups" (p. 147).

[25] See for example *The Public and Its Problems*, pp. 166-184; *Individualism, Old and New* (1929), *John Dewey, The Later Works, 1925-1953*, vol. 5, edited by Jo Ann Boydston (Carbondale: Southern Illinois University Press, 1984): pp. 50-65; *Ethics, The Later Works*, vol. 7, pp. 358-366; and *Liberalism and Social Action* (1935), *John Dewey, The Later Works, 1925-1953*, vol. 11, edited by Jo Ann Boydston (Carbondale: Southern Illinois University Press, 1987): pp. 23-40.

[26] Dewey, *The Public and Its Problems*, p. 167.

[27] Dewey, *Liberalism and Social Action, The Later Works*, vol. 11, p. 56.
[28] Dewey, *Ethics, The Later Works,* vol. 7, p. 358.

CRITICISMS OF DEWEY'S PHILOSOPHY: EFFECTIVE POWER?

As I pointed out in the last chapter, character signifies the way in which social power is directed, controlled, and converted into particular ends. More specifically, character refers to the forming and measuring of the ends of action according to their effects on the growth of the individual's interest and skill, as well as upon the specific conditions set up in consequence that influence the active participation and development of others. Thus, estimates of power as either enhancing or debilitating are all one with some character defining and judging the moral significance of acts according to his or her idea of the good to be served and the right and wrong way to serve it. However, differences in the range and thoroughness of judgment result in differences in the estimates of power. As Dewey points out, "The fact that the idea or principle of right has such a natural basis and inevitable role does not, however, signify that it will not conflict with what an individual judges to be his good and his end, nor does it guarantee the rightfulness of all claims and demands that are put forth in its name."[1] How, then, should conflicts of right be settled, according to Dewey?

Conflicting claims of right should be settled according to the same standard intrinsic to any act of human judgment: the degree to which those particular things exacted contribute to a wider, more meaningful idea of the good and sharpen perceptions of the responsibilities necessary to bring about this good. Furthermore, Dewey's ideal of democracy entails a method by which to settle conflicts and guide social action. Insofar as the aim is to expand and unify habit in a way such that others may share in this good by directing their own growth with more meaning, then, the ideal requires constant communication guided by kindness, sincerity, and fairness. The ideal demands that individuals work together in good faith in order to identify sources of conflict, judge actual and potential effects of action (power), and form an idea of good that benefits all. Dewey's critics, however, charge that his criterion and method for settling conflicts are flawed and naïve.

Although all of Dewey's critics share the idea that his philosophical assumptions are the root of this problem, they do not point to the same assumptions. In fact, Dewey's critics fall into three groups. The first group claims that Dewey's materialist philosophy undercuts enduring, transcendent principles. In effect of Dewey's metaphysical stance, this group of critics suggests, individuals are left in insoluble struggles to assert their various claims of right over others without any overarching, authoritative criteria to which to appeal. Thus, shared experience becomes a cesspool of coercion, manipulation, and deceit. The second group of critics points out that Dewey's attempt to synthesize Hegelian ontology with the biological theses of Darwin locks Dewey into a deterministic, evolutionary progression that portrays social unity as a certainty over time and reason as a shared function of human adaptation ubiquitously driving toward the ultimate realization of this unity. The second group of critics suggests that since his biological framework precludes an account of interest and desire as significant factors guiding human attention, Dewey fails to see how reason can be used to dominate—and liberate—others. According to these critics, then, Dewey's Hegelian informed biological framework unwittingly covers up the human influence in perpetuating social injustice and leaves his political ideas meaningless.

The third and most challenging group of critics maintains that Dewey's method of solving social conflicts rests upon two naïve assumptions. First, Dewey assumes that those who come in conflict over values do so in the good faith of resolving the conflict with a broader, cooperative interest in mind. Second, Dewey assumes that reason aimed at illuminating how ideas and practices stand in the way of forging a more equal and cooperative experience is a sufficient method for solving social conflict. This third group of critics suggests that Dewey simply cannot account for the deep-seated desires of people to control and to be controlled. Furthermore, he fails to see that unfair social arrangements exist that allow individuals to manipulate the means of communication in order to secure selfish interests while masking this selfishness through appeals to freedom, equality, and cooperation. By unjustly influencing the ways in which individuals come together to identify and judge ends of share activity, those who benefit from unfair social relations further cultivate the conditions that form and nourish the interests, desires, affections, and habits that make up individual character. These critics argue that Dewey fails to see how particular social arrangements produce individual characters whose unwitting but eager service to the interest of a few debilitates the actual opportunities for personal and social growth. Thus, according to these critics, Dewey's failure to account for how debilitating sources of power work through and possess individual consciousness leaves his idea of cooperative inquiry as an oversimplistic, ineffective means for dealing with these controlling forces. While all of Dewey's critics suggest that he does not understand how powerful ill-will poisons the method which, in turn, undermines the normative prescription of the ideal, their reasons why Dewey is blind to power warrants a closer look at each criticism.

FIRST CRITICISM: LOVEJOY, CROSSER, AND KIRK

The first group of Dewey's critics, including Arthur Lovejoy, Paul Crosser, and Russell Kirk, claims that Dewey holds strictly to a 19th Century empiricist tradition of metaphysical and epistemological realism. These critics suggest that by assuming the old empiricist stance, Dewey inherits a conceptual framework that cannot explain how the human mind forms ideas about the non-phenomenal past and future. Without correcting this inherent epistemological flaw, Dewey cannot explain how mere physical sensations of present matter (the bedrock of the empiricist epistemology) are spatially and temporally cross-referenced with each other to form a continuum of organized conduct. At best, then, it seems that

Dewey's epistemological assumptions are inconsistent with and do not justify his having any social and political ideals at all, as Arthur Lovejoy implies. At worst, as Crosser and Kirk claim, Dewey's brand of empiricism denies outright the existence of a spiritual realm, leaving human beings trapped within their inner worlds of disjointed sensations and cursing social experience with an extreme relativism that undercuts the objective authority of enduring moral principles.

By far, the most detailed and technical of the critics who develop this criticism is Arthur Lovejoy. In *The Thirteen Pragmatisms*, Lovejoy claims that Dewey's ideas about meaning and truth are faulty because they develop out of his erroneous idea that the physical sensations of objects are necessary before thoughts of these objects can occur. Lovejoy associates Dewey with an "immediatism" in which "experience does not consist of mental states which duplicate things, but simply of things."[2] Now, "immediatism" is another name for the 19th Century empiricist assumption that direct sensory impressions are the only means of definite contact with and certainty of phenomena. As I have pointed out in Chapter Two of this study, the empiricists maintained that abstract representations of phenomena not produced by direct sense are indefinite, inadmissible, and therefore non-existent. Also pointed out in Chapter Two, the empiricist idea of reason amounted to nothing more than a mere register of immediately sensed matter.[3] According to Lovejoy, this immediatism serves as the unifying principle of the more encompassing "radical empiricism" that Dewey inherits from William James.

> Radical empiricism. . . .is a doctrine about knowledge which, when consistent, characteristically ignores time and temporal distinctions. It is a philosophy of the instantaneous. The moving spring of its dialectic is a feeling that knowledge means immediacy, that an existent is strictly known only insofar as it is given, present, actually possessed in a definite bit of concrete experience.[4]

Lovejoy suggests that if Dewey is to remain consistent with the logic of his empiricist stance, he cannot develop the function of reason to be anything more than the inventory of felt objects in their immediate spatial relation with each other. That is, Dewey cannot account for how the human mind in fact goes from the immediate sense of objects to what Lovejoy calls the "trans-empirical" phases of remembered past and inferred future by way of these objects. Without the ability to form ideas that represent sensations not directly present, the human mind cannot retain, distinguish, associate, and organize its various experiences into a coherent system of meaning. The effect, then, if Dewey remains consistent with his empiricist roots, is an individual locked within the subjective realm of unconnected feelings without the mental equipment to plan and act according to the demands of his environment.[5] Lovejoy, however, suggests that Dewey does not stay consistent, since his theories of meaning and truth do not follow from his most basic epistemological premise.

According to Lovejoy, Dewey develops a concept of meaning that consists of the future anticipated consequences for conduct, illuminated all at once in the direct sensation of immediate objects.[6] For example, a baby's cry signifies hunger to his attentive mother and suggests to her the need to nourish him. The truth or validity of the cry signifying hunger and thus nourishment is confirmed insofar as the anticipated consequences are realized through the ensuing action. As Lovejoy understands it, Dewey's idea of truth refers to "the complete realization of the experience (or series of experiences) to which the judgment had antecedently pointed. . . .The criterion of the truth of a judgment is its satisfactoriness as such."[7] Lovejoy suggests that since Dewey's idea of the mind is incapable of retaining and selectively recalling previous experience, it has no store of knowledge by which to test the validity of a proposed meaning before acting upon it. According to Lovejoy, Dewey's "expost facto theory of truth" fails to provide general principles to guide human conduct and therefore is functionally meaningless. "Our intellect is condemned, according to this doctrine, to subsist wholly by a system of deferred payments; it gets no cash down."[8] Lovejoy, furthermore, points out that Dewey does not develop a concept of the human mind capable of making inferences from bare sensory data to anticipated consequences. Therefore, upon the logic of his epistemological premises, Dewey should not have been able to develop theories of meaning and truth at all.[9]

In light of what he takes to be Dewey's inconsistencies, Lovejoy points to Dewey's ideas about meaning and truth as evidence of a metaphysical realism underlying Dewey's work in which physical data are assumed to cohere already in a predetermined system of relations. While Lovejoy acknowledges that Dewey includes "consciousness," "reflection," and "inference" as native and constant in experience, Lovejoy understands Dewey to be saying that these cognitive processes are inherent to the mere physiological effect of present stimuli. Thus, the inference of things not present, such as future consequences, is intrinsic and automatic in the sensing of present data.[10] According to Lovejoy's understanding of this account, the meaning of the phenomenal world is given in the immediate flash of the moment upon the senses, the validity of which only becomes verified through the further perception of moments as they unfold. Inconsistencies and conflicts between anticipated consequences and actual outcomes do occur, but these may be attributed to an inevitable lag in human perception. Lovejoy suspects that in order for Dewey to develop such an account as this from his barren immediatist assumption, he had to assume a metaphysical stance that would give dynamic coherence to the mere sensation of physical data.

> What I have called the theory of expost facto nature of truth is a somewhat blurred reflection of a certain metaphysical doctrine which, although not always very explicitly put forward, . . .is the doctrine of the "open-ness" of the future, and of the determinative or "creative" efficacy of each "present" moment in the ever-transient process of conscious judgment, choice, and action. The two parts of the doctrine obviously enough go together: if the process truly brings into being at each new moment a genuinely new and unique increment of reality, then, so long as any moment's increment has not yet been brought forth, it cannot yet be called in any intelligible sense real; and if, similarly, the thing that is to be is a sheer nonentity until it enters into actual, temporal experience, the moment in which it becomes an experience

must be credited within the creation ex nihilo of a new item of being. . . .Such a metaphysics appears to imply the partial contingency and (from the standpoint of any "present" knowledge) indeterminateness of the future content of reality. . . .The future may be. . . .regarded as presenting to our understanding only a narrow margin of the unpredictable; its general character and the greater mass of its content may be supposed, without departing from the conception in question, to be predetermined by the accumulated and crystallized results of reality up to date, of which any possible future and novel increment of being must be the child, and to which it must be capable of accommodation.[11]

According to Lovejoy's account, then, there are two possible ways to read Dewey's epistemological assumptions: either as an oversimplistic idea of the human mind that reduces though to bare feeling or as a by-product of a metaphysical realism in which the meaning and truth of the phenomenal world depend solely upon individual perception. As Paul Crosser sees it, either way amounts to a "cognitive indeterminableness."[12]

Similarly to Lovejoy's argument, Crosser claims that Dewey's oversimplistic reliance upon the physical senses precludes mental representation of past experiences that allows the individual to reflect upon and abstract ideas of those experiences pertinent to guiding present conduct. Crosser suggests that Dewey's empiricism flattens the individual's ability to make qualitative distinctions and thus leads to a "cognitive indefiniteness" in which judgments between valid and invalid perceptions of meaning are impossible. "The end result at which Dewey arrives in both cases is essentially the same, it amounts to a denial of the feasibility to draw a cognitive distinction between fictitious and non-fictitious propositions."[13] Although Crosser does not fully work out the social implications of what he sees as "cognitive indefiniteness," he does imply that its logical conclusion is moral relativism.

Dewey's philosophy in all its major aspects constitutes an attempt to destroy all philosophy. In that sense, Dewey undertook a monumental task. The success of his undertaking, however, was to have the many Americans who came under his influence without any generalized outlook on life. It left the American intellectual at large, as well as the American artist, with a fragmentary view of things, it left, in particular, the American teacher enmeshed in unrelated details. . . .Dewey has deprived those Americans who have come under his influence of a general framework within which they could place their everyday activities. Dewey has made America lose its perspective. . . .Dewey has descended to a position of extreme relativism which constitutes the ultimate destination on the road to cognitive indeterminableness.[14]

Whatever Crosser may lack in spelling out the social implications of Dewey's so called empiricism, Russell Kirk certainly takes up the task in explicit manner. Kirk lumps Dewey's "naturalism" into a host of radical traditions hell bent upon undercutting belief in a "divine intent" for society and, therefore, dismantling eternal moral principles necessary to judge right and wrong conduct.[15]   Although failing to provide philosophical explication of his claims about Dewey, Kirk's understanding of Dewey's work seems to be in line with that of Lovejoy's and Crosser's: "a thoroughgoing naturalism. . . .denying the whole realm of spiritual values: nothing exists but physical sensation, and life has no aims but physical satisfaction."[16]   While Lovejoy suggests that Dewey's epistemological stance leaves Dewey with no logical means for referring to and incorporating enduring principles for conduct, Kirk sees the upshot in a harsher way. Kirk suggests that Dewey's emphasis on physical satisfaction not only shows a thorough contempt for tradition and authority but results in a hedonism in which the greatest pleasure for the greatest number is the moral law. According to Kirk, this hedonism renders the belief in man's "natural proclivity toward violence and sin" meaningless and, thus, destroys all means by which to judge between right and wrong satisfactions.[17]

If this group of critics is correct, it is not much of a logical stretch to say that Dewey should not have been able to develop an idea of conflict in the first place, to say nothing of a criterion and method for settling conflict. That Dewey does develop social and political insights indicates an underlying realism to these critics that slips in philosophical merit because it rests upon an immediatist epistemology. According to these critics' accounts, Dewey leaves the meaning and truth of all things, especially those socially and morally most significant, captive within the subjective feelings of the single individual without any means to determine if these feelings correctly correspond to the objective circumstances of the case. Therefore, Dewey's criterion for judging the truth of circumstances amounts to the feeling of satisfaction relative to each individual, according to Crosser. This cognitive relativism translates into a hedonism, as Kirk sees it, such that expanding the number of physical satisfactions serves as the moral ideal and standard. The result is a social experience shot through with competing satisfactions and no objective, overarching criteria by which to settle social conflicts justly.

SECOND CRITICISM: MILLS AND DIGGINS

The second group of Dewey's critics, represented by C. Wright Mills and John Patrick Diggins, suggests that Dewey uses a biological framework derived from the work of Darwin to restate his Hegelian assumptions. These critics point out that this synthesis of Hegel and Darwin leads Dewey to see human experience as an inevitable progression towards the ultimate unity of all existence. According to Mills, Dewey understands the catalyst of this march to be the human organism organically struggling with its environment to perfect a more balanced adjustment. Employing "the biologic-adjustment model of action," as Mills puts it, Dewey is forced into a narrow social and political perspective.[18] That is, given the logic of his biological model, Dewey has to develop an idea of reason as a simple stimulus-response behavior, lacking in what Mills calls the constitutive capacity to envision and judge a prospective plan of action. Furthermore, Dewey is required to portray conflict only in terms of the isolated individual's struggle against nature, excluding struggles over value between human beings altogether. John Patrick Diggins points out that Dewey does include social conflict as an inherent part of nature. However, Diggins claims that Dewey's idea of social conflict is one of necessary but temporary maladjustment of opposites awaiting automatic adjustment into a greater unity through the application of value-neutral reason. According to these critics, the formality of Dewey's biological model not only hides social conflict over value but also diverts necessary attention away from the particular interests involved. Therefore, these critics suggest, Dewey's work unwittingly perpetuates social injustice by providing a metaphysical excuse for those who benefit from unequal relations of power in times of conflict.

In *Sociology and Pragmatism*, Mills suggests that Dewey formulates the Hegelian concepts of "the Absolute" and "the dialectic" in Darwinian terms in order to overcome the epistemological problems inherent to the rationalist philosophical tradition.[19] As Mills indicates, the rationalist stance suffered from the traditional mind and matter dualism. More specifically, as I have pointed out in Chapter Two of this study, the rationalists' problem had been one of explaining how eternal forms given to human beings as innate ideas cause a coherent sensory experience through time and space. Kant had argued that this epistemological problem could be cleared up by maintaining that sensory experience is necessary to evoke and give body to these otherwise abstract forms. The problem with Kant's epistemological account, however, was that he provided no means whereby human beings could be certain that their finite experience was a manifestation of the unconditioned realm. This left the idea of an eternal transcendent realm a matter of empirically unwarranted speculation. Furthermore, if the universal forms were immutable and given to all human beings by means of innate ideas, Kant failed to explain how and why those sharing the same finite relations come into conflict over meaning within their experience.[20] As successor to Kant in the rationalist tradition, Hegel inherited Kant's philosophical problems.

For his part, Hegel assumed Kant's idea of a transcendent realm of unconditioned meaning, which Hegel called the Universal Absolute. Hegel also maintained that the ideas making up the Absolute are made concrete only as they are realized through the particular actions of individuals. Unlike Kant, Hegel emphasized that the Absolute consists of the relations of all phenomena, including all agreements and contradictions, and, thus, refers to the ultimate unity of all difference. Furthermore, Hegel dropped the idea that the whole of the Absolute is given a priori to human beings in the form of innate ideas. Hegel argued that individuals' particular experiences are partial manifestations of the Absolute, which require their opposite manifestations in order to provide a fuller understanding of the whole and which individuals come to understand only in retrospect. Conceptualizing the transcendent realm in this way, Hegel could account for the occurrence of difference and conflict among individuals' perceptions and understandings of their particular experiences. According to Hegel, then, the Absolute can be understood only as it is manifested and built up in parts through human interaction and conflict. Thus, Hegel made conflict and change (the Hegelian dialectic) ontological and epistemological necessities. Although Mills does not work out a full explication of Hegel, his quotation and acceptance of George Herbert Mead's understanding of Hegel seems to be consistent with the interpretation of Hegel developed in this present study.

> The Hegelian statement of thought is of the tradition known as Absolute or Objective Idealism. . . .The entire universe is to Hegel the expression of the thought of the supermind. "In the philosophy of Hegel the development of mind is the same thing as the development of the world.". . .Thus, within his Universal Mind, or Rational Process, the opposition which gives rise to thought is an opposition of two universals. The relation of things is a relation of thought; the cognitive relation is ubiquitous, and in "Nature." Ideas come to be opposed with each other. In the mind of the cosmic self, they come to be opposed. And the development of the universe, of an insect, of a rock, is a process of resolving contradictions. All thinking, says Hegel, begins "when unity has disappeared from the life of man, and when its oppositions, having lost their vital relations and interactions assert themselves as independent."[21]

Mills suggests that while Dewey apparently rejects the Absolute as a formal concept, he accepts Hegel's notion that human action is a partial manifestation of a totality of relations that requires conflict between opposites for its further concrete realization and understanding. In order to rid himself of Hegel's dualistic problems, Mills suggests, Dewey abandons Hegel's language altogether. According to Mills, Dewey channels the Hegelian dialectic through "the acceptance of certain implications drawn from the biological work of 'Darwin,' i.e., a set of biologically oriented psychological theses later to be known as Behaviorism."[22] Mills does not work out explicitly and systematically what these biological theses are. However, an analysis of Mills' claim that Dewey simply reads the Hegelian dialectic into the biological theses of Darwin provides an idea of how Mills sees Dewey understanding these theses: the human being as a natural organism struggling for survival against the demands of nature and the outcome of this natural struggle as an adapted response more suited to meet environmental demands.[23]

According to Mills, Dewey wants to avoid the two-world dualism inherent to the rationalist metaphysical and epistemological stance but wants to portray the individual as part of a continuous whole. Seizing upon the idea of the human organism as an organic part of nature, Dewey argues that nature itself is the continuous whole out of which everything springs and back into which everything merges. Understanding nature to be the organized whole of all relations, including all opposites, Dewey then can account for the finite quality of the organism's ontological and epistemological status without referring to a realm outside of this experience. In keeping with the Hegelian dialectic, Dewey suggests that the ontological existence of the human organism is one of necessary conflict and resolution with the specific demands of its environment such that the effect is an ever-refined integration between the two. From this biological framework, Dewey maintains that the finite actions of the human organism are simply the partial manifestation of the totality of all natural relations. According to Mills, Dewey "naturalizes" the Absolute such that he has a metaphysical basis to make the claim that human reason is a derived and secondary response to nature.[24]

As Mills understands it, Dewey maintains that the specific conditions of an individual's environment pressure and strain the individual into a simple physiological response characteristic of all organic instincts to survive. The specific conditions pose obstacles for the organism's on-going activity, its continued survival, and thus, directly determine the qualitative nature its response.[25] That is, environmental change acts as a "problematic situation" that drives the organism to adjust its on-going behavior to conform to the particular facts at hand or to succumb to them. The metaphysical implication is that the organism's response either way simply is the concrete manifestation of nature revealing its difference amidst its unity.

From within the finite experience of the human organism, however, this adjustment proceeds by way of trial and error behavior such that every action and reaction ultimately results in a successive stage of biological equilibrium incrementally better than the last.[26] Thus, according to Mills, Dewey develops human thought as a behavioral by-product (a secondary variation) of the stimulus-response cycle between the environment and the human organism.

> All thought is intrinsically bound up with and conditioned by, though secondary to and derived from, the larger context of non-reflective experiences and behaviors. . . .This context "may most easily be described from a negative point of view: it is a type of experience which cannot be called a knowledge experience." Dewey, operating on a formal level, is concerned with a revolt against formalistic positions. Hence, in logical contexts, there is no focus upon, no detailed and empirical characterization of, this "non-cognitive context" of thought. Such "experience" is conceived in formal terms, left empirically residual. All revolts to a greater or lesser measure participate in, take something from, that against which they constitute a revolt. The experiential context of thought is conceived as in itself internally organized. Its organization is of a "non-logical character." It is "objectively continuous and organized," and has "infinite range of context" and specific moving "focus." The situation wherein thought is located evokes thought, and "determines its object." In the passage from non-reflective to and through reflective modes of experience there is fundamental continuity.[27]

Mills does not work out an exact, systematic account of Dewey's concept of reason. He claims that Dewey's biological framework leaves the function of reason ambiguous and formal. In the most general sense, therefore, Mills states that to Dewey, reason is a "response to a specific stimulus condition," the function of which amounts, at best, to a mere descriptive cataloging of experienced change up to date and helping "in the overt manipulation of physical objects."[28] Mills suggests that Dewey never specifies exactly how reason is to help in biological adjustment. Mills also implies that since Dewey understands human development to be an inevitable process of nature, he does not develop reason to include judgment about the qualitative differences in consequence of action and, thus, leaves out altogether what Mills calls the "constitutive" function of thought. That is, the idea of a predetermined plan of natural adjustment makes it unnecessary for the human organism to develop a mental function that formulates ends and means, anticipates consequences, and deliberates over the proper course of action to take. Thus, according to Mills, the formality of Dewey's biological framework presents value-decisions as an epistemological impossibility and in effect hides actual discrepancies between individuals over value.

> The simple fact of the matter is that the statement on every other page of Dewey to the effect that men adjust by means of reflection is never tentatively handled in a genuinely empirical manner. What empirical support is adduced is squeezed into the biological framework. The biological model of action, "adaptation," by its formality enables one to avoid value-decisions. The biological terms in which it is advanced aids the tacit assumption of cultural sanctions of activity of a certain kind. . . .By treating as real or at least central only that action which manipulates physical objects we are drawn to the view that the function of all action is mutual adaptation between organisms and environment. By putting the matter in biological terms, it is formalized, which is to say that the content of the end of action (and of reflection) is left open. Adaptation is the term in Dewey which stands at this level. By its usage, value-decisions as value-decisions are assimilated into the biological and hidden by formality.[29]

Exactly thirty years after the publication of Mills' criticism, John Patrick Diggins makes virtually the same claim about Dewey in *The Promise of Pragmatism*.[30] Diggins suggests that Dewey synthesizes ideas from Darwin and Hegel as a way not only to solve the traditional philosophical dualism between spirit and matter but also to heal "an inward laceration" that Dewey keenly feels as a result of the mounting conflict between science and religion. Diggins claims that Dewey holds to the Darwinian idea of the human being as an organic creature of natural evolution. He suggests that Dewey then draws upon Hegel in order to work out the "philosophical meaning" of the evolutionary process.

By way of Hegel, Diggins maintains, Dewey understands natural evolution to be predicated upon inherent conflict as the necessary generator of all change toward the ultimate unity of all reality. As Diggins puts it, "The idea that reality must be seen as a continuity between matter and spirit, emotion and reason, mind and society, and that all reality, the bad together with the good, is part of a process of inner and external struggle toward the realization of its own free and ultimate being, left a permanent impression on Dewey."[31] Furthermore, Diggins suggests that the synthesis of Darwin and Hegel allows Dewey to account for social conflicts as necessary but temporary stages in natural evolution. Dewey therefore can explain, for example, the divisiveness of the Civil War and the feelings of existential doubt and angst symptomatic of the scientific challenge to entrenched religious faith as inevitable by-products of nature. He also can maintain with optimism that these conflicts inevitably will be resolved through time. Similar to

Mills' account, Diggins claims that Dewey sees human reason as a behavioral by-product of adaptation that functions to facilitate human solidarity and the completion of natural unity.[32]

Diggins suggests that Dewey understands the function of reason to be the organic process by which the human being comes to a greater awareness of and thus a more refined control over all natural change. According to Diggins, Dewey sees the specific circumstances of the individual's environment directing the quality and extent of his mental growth. The inevitable change of the individual's circumstances develops and tests his abilities to analyze, imagine, judge, and control natural change itself. To Dewey, Diggins suggests, reason serves as the means to formulate and revise ideas as plans for action, to anticipate and judge the consequences of ideas, and to choose between these consequences as ends for action.[33] On the one hand, then, Diggins points out that Dewey develops reason to include both analytic and synthetic functions. On the other hand, Diggins claims that Dewey's Hegelian-influenced ontological stance undercuts all mental functions that Dewey attributes to the human being in the first place.

As Diggins reads him, Dewey presents the ontological existence of man in nature as a "unilateral" progression in which nature dictates the particular conditions according to which man must align himself for his continual survival. This alignment requires the abilities to formulate, judge, and revise ideas as plans for action. However, according to Diggins, these abilities fall under the more general survival capacity of perceiving the similarities between present circumstances and those experienced and adjusted to in the past. That is, a present problem stimulates the individual to analyze his or her immediate circumstances in order to find similarities with some past experience. This analysis suggests ideas for action, and, thus, the individual acts. In turn, the truth or worth of the idea depends upon the individual's judgment of the degree of stability, definiteness, and unity actually brought about in consequence of the response. The individual therefore revises his or her response in light of his or her judgment. In turn, he or she gains a more sensitive and thorough control over his or her ability to adjust to the process of natural change. According to Diggins, however, Dewey's ontological stance forces him into an idea of truth that consists in a measurement of validity and reliability that can be taken only after the fact of action. Therefore, ideas do not have any regulative authority for judgments about conduct beforehand.

According to Diggins, Dewey's epistemological—and ensuing ethical—problems stem from his portrayal of human beings as creatures in constant need to adjust themselves to the whims of nature rather than as creatures desiring to modify their environment according to self-determined interests. "Darwinism, of course, made Dewey aware that nature continually challenges man's capacity for survival, and historically man has responded to the challenge with magic, rituals, gods, and scientific intelligence. Yet this emphasis on control can be narrowly unilateral, positing man as always responsive rather than deliberative, a creature of need rather than desire."[34] By suggesting that human reason develops as a mere response in direct proportion to changing environmental stimuli, Dewey ultimately portrays human reason as an impotent capacity for dealing with the future uncertainties of change itself.

> Dewey remained convinced that mind is an organ created by its function because he refused to regard mind as something distinct from nature. Others would attribute to "instinct" the qualities Dewey attributed to intelligence, for many of the endowments of the animal and human world—the eye, the bird's wing, the sense of smell, and the like—evolved as elementary prehensions in the evolutionary processes from which it developed. Thus his conviction that what the mind knows is conditioned by what it experiences has profound implications for the problems of truth and authority. To the extent that the thought processes of mind derive from experience, thought itself cannot escape the contingencies of experience in order to provide regulative principles of knowledge, not to mention immutable ideas and universal truths.[35]

Diggins suggests that as a result of his Darwinian-Hegelian framework, Dewey is locked logically into accepting an idea of social and political experience that rests upon the belief that the process of evolution itself provides all the moral good necessary to resolve social conflict into greater social unity.[36] That is, Dewey sees social activity as an inherent part of natural evolution, since the end of the evolutionary process is the realization of a complete human solidarity and community. Thus, as Diggins understands him, Dewey sees human obligation and duty as the continual development of the individual's capacities to adapt in a way that is congruent with the development of the ultimate good of natural unity as it is embodied generally in social laws. Since there is only one regulating value for all nature to be fulfilled, social conflict to Dewey cannot be a dispute over the value of consequences as a result of human development. Diggins implies that Dewey understands social conflict to be the concrete manifestation of nature revealing its constituent contradictions. The social purpose of reason, then, is to identify underlying ideas as the sources of opposition, determine their consequences under past circumstances, and illuminate how these sources should be revised and balanced in light of the ultimate good as it has been revealed through the process of change up to date. Therefore, the social and political problem is not a matter of adjudicating between competing interests and opposing claims of right; the problem simply is a matter of unifying opposing groups according to the natural plan illuminated by reason.

As pointed out above, Diggins maintains that Dewey's ontological position undercuts any constitutive functions that Dewey attributes to human reason. Diggins claims that Dewey bases his social and political perspective on the naïve idea that reason can disclose the principles of unity underlying all natural change and therefore point out the indisputable direction necessary for further human—and social—development. Diggins points out that Dewey "claimed cognitive abilities in politics that his epistemology denied in philosophy."[37] Furthermore, Diggins suggests that by aiming at the process of change, reason cannot suggest any particular goods other than change itself and the general ability to adjust to it.

Therefore, value decisions and discrepancies about specific ends of action are hidden by the language of biological adaptation. Thus, according to Diggins, Dewey can assume that social conflict is just a matter of maladjustment to the natural course of social development and that when this underlying course is illuminated by reason, all opposing groups automatically (naturally) will accept it. Diggins suggests that Dewey's biological framework precludes him from conceptualizing reason as developing by way of particular desires and interests. Thus, Dewey cannot see how reason might serve in the realization of selfish desires that set up unequal social relations and exploit others in consequence.[38]

> Dewey not only refused to give much attention to power and its origins, he also had no idea where to look for it other than as some kind of aberration. When Dewey thought at all about power—not as the ability to act and have effect but as control and domination—he usually interpreted it as an example of dislocation and maladjustment, the failure of education and intelligence to catch up with economic development and the rise of big business. . . .Dewey came close to suggesting that the evils of power would disappear to the extent that the individual merges with the social and members of a democratic society lead lives of mutuality as an "organic whole."[39]

According to both Mills and Diggins, Dewey's biological framework fails to account sufficiently for the development and divergence of self-defined interests (ends) as these emerge in relation to specific contextual demands. Unable to find a place for self-defined interests within this framework, Dewey has to develop human reason as a benign function of the evolutionary process itself. Therefore, these critics suggest, Dewey not only fails to account adequately for social conflict as the struggle between competing interests but ignores the use of reason in perpetuating further social injustice by those who already benefit from unequal social relations. Furthermore, as Dewey critic Reinhold Niebuhr suggests and as Diggins implies, by portraying social conflicts as necessary but temporary stages in an evolutionary progression, Dewey diverts analytic attention away from the concrete causes of social struggles. In effect of his idea of social conflict as necessary but temporary, Dewey legitimizes conflict and the relations of power set up in consequence as inevitable and natural phases of evolution.[40]

THIRD CRITICISM: MARCUSE, RYDER, ESTREMERA, AND FLAY

Stemming from his general criticism of middle-class liberalism, Reinhold Niebuhr argues that Dewey's concept of democracy, like all liberal concepts of democracy, suffers from an oversimplistic view of human nature. Niebuhr's argument not only echoes the first two lines of criticism already developed but also ties these in with the third line of argument against Dewey. Similar to the first group of critics, Niebuhr suggests that Dewey develops a naturalism that undercuts all transcendent principles governing human nature, including the idea of "original sin." This move, according to Niebuhr, leads Dewey to ignore the evil of selfishness as an inherent limitation of human nature. (Niebuhr furthermore suggests that Dewey's naturalism leaves Dewey without any stable philosophical ground upon which he can argue for the necessity of democracy as the best moral guide for human conduct.) Along the lines of the second group of critics, Niebuhr points out that Dewey modifies his naturalism according to the assumptions he inherits from the rationalist tradition. Dewey's naturalized Hegelianism (what Niebuhr simply refers to as liberalism) leads Dewey to portray human experience as an inevitable progression towards a fuller social unity and justice, hastened about through the always-benign use of human intelligence.

> The cultural foundation of western democracy is eighteenth—and nineteenth—century liberalism. This liberalism rests upon rationalistic optimism. It believes that it is comparatively easy to "substitute reason for force" and that mankind is embarked on a progressive development which will substitute "free cooperative inquiry" for political partisanship and social conflict. It regards the peculiar ambitions and desires of races and nations as irrationalities which must gradually yield to universal values, generally recognized and established by reason, that is, by some kind of disincarnate reason of pure objectivity. Democracy, in other words, rests upon a faith in the essential goodness of man and the possibility of completely rational behavior.[41]

According to Niebuhr, Dewey is too optimistic in his presentation of human beings as naturally cooperative and blind to selfishness as an inherent character flaw of human nature. In effect, Dewey fails to account for "predatory self-interest" as an underlying cause for individuals to manipulate and control others through intelligence. Niebuhr suggests that Dewey' theory, like all liberal theories of human nature and reason, "hardly does justice to the complexities of human behavior and to the inevitable conflicts between the objectives determined by reason and those of the total body of impulse, rationally unified but bent upon more immediate goals than those which man's highest reason envisages. Men may achieve a rational unity of impulse around the organizing center of the possessive instinct or will-to-power, and yet have a faint sense of obligation to achieve social objectives, which transcend, or are in conflict with, their will-to-power."[42] Therefore, by ignoring self-interest as an undermining factor to any cooperative effort aimed at a greater social justice, Dewey's argument for a democratic ideal and method is naïve. The third group of Dewey's critics develops this latter idea to which Niebuhr calls attention.

Herbert Marcuse, John Ryder, Joseph Flay, and Miguel Estremera maintain that Dewey's overly optimistic faith in human cooperation and goodwill leads him to underestimate the human desire to exploit others for the sake of selfish profit. Therefore, as Marcuse and Ryder suggest, Dewey attributes social conflict to a simple maladjustment of values (cultural lag) capable of just solution by means of shared inquiry and the free and open exchange of ideas. As Flay and Estremera point out, since Dewey fails to recognize depravity as a constituent part of social experience, he fails to account for how individuals corrupt the means of cooperative inquiry and communication. In turn, Dewey develops no insight into the particular ways in which powerful, ill-willed individuals structure social conditions such that others unwittingly desire to serve the interests of the few and come to legitimize their own subjugation as reasonable and natural. In light of this defect, Dewey's method for enhancing social justice seems a naïve, oversimplistic means for fighting the forces of power that preempt a flourishing democratic experience.

In "John Dewey's *Theory of Valuation*," Herbert Marcuse sees Dewey suggesting that all human desires entail ends and means that may be subject to empirical test and judged as to their reasonableness or unreasonableness.[43] As Marcuse points out, Dewey draws the distinction between reasonable and unreasonable desires according to the degree to which desires are formed through a consideration of their consequences within particular existential contexts. That is, in Dewey's words, "'The difference between reasonable and unreasonable desires and interests is precisely the difference between those which arise casually and are not reconstituted through consideration of the conditions that will actually decide the outcome and those which are formed on the basis of existing liabilities and potential resources.'"[44] According to Marcuse, Dewey thinks that collective identification and judgment of conflicting desires will expose those that are reasonable and congruent with the historical efforts of human kind to bring about greater freedom and those that are unreasonable and serve to protect the privileges of a special class. Furthermore, Marcuse suggests that Dewey believes that shared inquiry and deliberation alone will lead automatically to a reexamination of desires, the necessary effect of which will be the release of individual capacities fueled by a desire for ends that will be beneficial to all.

According to Marcuse, Dewey's method for the revaluation of conflicting desires rests upon two naïve assumptions. First, as Marcuse implies, Dewey assumes that those who come into conflict over values do so in the good faith of resolving the conflict so as to bring about a freer, more cooperative and equitable social experience. Assuming that humankind is essentially good, Dewey further assumes that individuals who come to cross-purposes do so not out of selfish or malicious intent. They come to conflict due to the natural variance of interests cultivated in response to differing social conditions or because individuals have not properly thought out the consequences of their interests on the particular conditions at hand. For example, the so-called captains of industry clash with organized labor. If Marcuse is correct about Dewey's assumptions, then the explanation for the conflict between management and labor must be simply that both groups have not properly considered the consequences of their respective claims in relation to the needs inherent to the existing circumstances. The assumption underlying this explanation is that members of both groups have the good intention of creating a better social experience but the as yet unmediated inconsistencies between their respective values impede them from doing so.

In an argument similar to Marcuse's, John Ryder states that Dewey refers to the idea of social conflict caused by unmediated inconsistencies as "cultural lag." As Ryder puts it, "The reason, on Dewey's view, that a society like ours has the serious economic, social and political problems that it does is that its material basis of production is no longer consistent with the ideas according to which it organizes itself."[45] In broader terms, Ryder's charge is that Dewey reduces all social conflict to the human failure to modify ideas to keep pace with changes in social practice and communication. Once individuals have the opportunity to become clear about matters of conflict, they will update their ideas to be consistent with the demands at hand. Thus, according to Ryder and Marcuse, Dewey's second naïve assumption follows from his first one.

As both Marcuse and Ryder understand him, Dewey claims that the only method needed to resolve discrepancies over value is cooperative discussion and inquiry. Once conflicting groups collectively work out the effects of each desire in terms of its potential liabilities and resources, both groups will reevaluate and modify their respective ends to include a broader social good. Ryder puts Dewey's idea of remedy this way:

> In order to solve society's problems we need to eradicate the cultural confusion and bring our ideology up to date. How do we accomplish this? We do it by clarifying the various and complex issues involved, by pointing out the fact of this "cultural lag" and by examining as clearly and rationally as possible those alternative solutions that best meet society's needs insofar as they are conducive to the ideals of genuine human community, freedom, and democracy. And to achieve this we must employ what Dewey calls the "method of intelligence." Since we are all to one extent or another party to the problems of our own society, the problems are thereby common ones. And since they are our common problems, the only appropriate way of dealing with them is through cooperative analysis and experimentation.[46]

On the basis of Dewey's criterion of reasonableness, stated above, Marcuse suggests that any desire may be legitimized as reasonable insofar as its social consequences are thought out in detail. As Marcuse puts it, "It is obvious that desires and interests may be found that are reasonable on this ground and still aim at oppression and annihilation."[47] Marcuse suggests—and Ryder concurs—that Dewey's fundamental problem is that he simply neglects the fact that human beings may become clear about the consequences of their interests but still choose to do evil.

> Should man become conscious of these antecedents, "is it not obvious that this knowledge of conditions and consequences would surely lead to revaluation of the desires and ends that had been assumed to be authoritative sources of valuation?" Unfortunately, it is not obvious at all. Dewey's optimism is characterized by a neglect of the existential contexts in which the authoritarian desires and interests live. The order that maintains the exclusive privileges of a "small group or special class" responds to deep-rooted desires, desires that are spread far beyond the governing strata. The desire for strong protection, the perverse lust for cruelty, the enjoyment of power over an impotent enemy and of liberation from the burden of autonomy, and numerous other desires that shaped the individual in the pre-history of fascism have been fulfilled to such an extent that, in comparison,

the desire of freedom seems to aim at some suicidal jump into nothing. The form of freedom that the run-of-the-mill individual has enjoyed in the past century must only strengthen the desire to abandon it, while the super human courage and loyalty of those who carry on their fight for freedom in the authoritarian states is "unreasonable" according to scientific standards: all consequences and all existing liabilities and resources speak against their efforts.[48]

Taking a different tack, Joseph Flay and Miguel Estremera point out that Dewey recognizes conflict caused by unequal social relations as part of the human condition. They also suggest that Dewey fully recognizes the desire of those who benefit from unequal social relations to keep these relations intact by actively opposing change. As Flay suggests in "Alienation and The Status Quo," "A spectre, recognized by Dewey himself, haunted his position almost from the beginning. It amounted to the realization that those in favor of or controlling the status quo will oppose anything which will mean a change in that status quo, at least in so far as it affects their position in the power hierarchy."[49] However, both of these critics claim that Dewey puts too much faith in the idea that face to face discussion between individuals will expose this opposition to change for what it is and force a synthesis of desires that promotes social growth. They suggest that Dewey's optimism about human cooperation blinds him to the dynamics and structure of power relations. Thus, as Flay and also Estremera argue, Dewey fails to understand the ways in which those guided by a desire for selfish profit use the means of communication to coerce a supporting consent from individuals to serve this selfish desire as a legitimate social good.

In *Democratic Theories of Hope*, Estremera suggests that Dewey correctly portrays social experience as the embodiment of shared habits.[50] As Estremera implies (and as pointed out explicitly in Chapter Four and Chapter Five of the present study) Dewey defines habit as the self-executing means by which individuals adjust themselves according to the demands of their particular environments. For Dewey, these demands always include the expectations of others to modify an activity in some qualitative sense. Expressed as claims of right, these demands pressure the individual to mediate his or her desires by reference to claims to happiness made by others who share in the consequences of the individual's activity. Again, as pointed out in Chapter Five of the present study, Dewey puts the ethical nature of the demands of others this way:

Others do not leave us alone. They actively express their estimates of good in demands made upon us. . . .When considered as claims and expectations, they constitute the Right in distinction from the Good. But their ultimate function and effect is to lead the individual to broaden his conception of the Good; they operate to induce the individual to feel that nothing is good for himself which is not also a good for others. They are stimuli to a widening of the area of consequences to be taken into account in forming ends and deducing what is Good.[51]

Estremera takes Dewey to be arguing that social change is directly proportional to the quality of demands on selfish desires to be mediated in a way that accounts for the happiness of others. In other words, Estremera understands Dewey to be saying, "Increase the exposure and criticism of selfish ends and bad habits will be self-corrected." Similar to Marcuse, Estremera suggests that what restricts Dewey's analysis of power is his insistence on "intellectualizing" the problem of social conflict. That is, Dewey assumes that once individuals are forced to confront the consequences of their ideas with rigor and clarity, the results will be a cooperative effort to produce the necessary conditions for a flourishing democratic experience.[52] Estremera maintains that Dewey's face to face method (which Estremera calls the "intersubjective approach") ignores the fact that individuals can—and do—manipulate the means of communication so as to affect the very conditions whereby others come to develop shared meanings and habits in the first place. Joseph Flay suggests that those who wish to establish social relations that maximize their personal benefit and minimize detection and conflict do so by various means of dissimulation. Simply put, Flay's claim is that Dewey does not account for dissimulation and deceit as part of the democratic method.

According to Flay, dissimulation includes the withholding of facts and evidence necessary for others to make thorough judgments while appearing, at the same time, to be free and open to public criticism and correction. The point of dissimulation is to create the invalid perception in others that the particular value at issue either does not conflict with the general good or will enhance the general good.

> In general, the reason for dissimulation is to restore or to bring about a situation in which what are in fact special interests and values appear to be either general interests and values, or at least, special interests which are not contrary to the general. Success in maintaining power concerning any given set of interests and values depends upon the appearance which the situation produces; the interests and values of the given group must at least appear not to exclude interests and values of other groups, either special or general. The optimum situation is one in which the group interests appear to agree with or promote the general interests.[53]

Once the particular value is perceived to be in harmony with the general good, those individuals who have a selfish interest in maintaining it act for its realization and then distribute the returns of the value in such a way that continues maximizing their personal profits while appearing to be beneficial to all. In turn, they claim that the value is essential to the objective realization of personal and social welfare. From the social point of view, the claim serves as a demand that the value be considered as a mediating factor among the whole system of social impulses. From the psychological point of view, the claim amounts to a demand that the value receive significant attention when considering personal needs, wants, and desires. Like all demands, the particular claim comes with a promise of rewards and punishments. If the value is not considered and supported, the result will be a withholding of the value, which is perceived to be essential to personal and social growth. However, the cause of the withholding will appear to be from the free choice of individuals whose decisions affect the objective circumstances that, in turn, will issue the detrimental consequences back to everyone. Thus, what appears to be free choice amounts to coercion by a specific group disguised as the workings of the objective conditions alone. As Flay points out, the ability to control the perceptions of others not only works to produce their consent but to disarm all opposition and to absorb all conflict.

> The reformer maintains that in his view the status quo is not really in the best interest of the majority of those concerned, and that the judgments of the latter constitute invalid perceptions of identification. At the same time, if a secure power position exists, the authentic conservative is able to agree with what the reformer has said and to mark the loss of the status quo a result of reformation. Thus far there is no disagreement between the reformers and authentic conservatives. But in addition to this, while the reformer marks the loss of the status quo as a positive result, the authentic conservative identifies it as a negative result. And it is the authentic conservative who controls the attention frame and therefore the interpretation of values. It therefore comes to this: "Follow the reformer and lose the status quo. Lose the status quo and lose all that which is most meaningful to you; for the status quo, the present value structure, will retaliate against the reformer's actions and you will suffer. The choice is yours." The reformer has been absorbed.[54]

According to both Flay and Estremera, Dewey simply does not account for dissimulation and deceit as contaminants of the democratic process. As Estremera suggests, "While Dewey does attack existing barriers to the democratic process, especially by the corporate sector, what he does not stress with enough gravity is their control of the institutional structure. This is an especially important point to address in reference to the limitations posited in the development of a public language."[55] By virtue of regulating shared habits, ill-willed individuals regulate the development of feelings, perceptions, wants and needs of others such that they come to desire ends that are antithetical to the growth of existing capacities and social equality. Estremera suggests that the recognition of this insidious type of power makes the idea of a free, open, and critical discussion of values problematic from the start.

> Thinking in itself becomes problematic due to the constant manipulation of the psyche by outside forces. What we feel may be genuine or autonomous intent on our part may be in reality an idea which is counter to that intent. The control and production of meaning at the institutional level in effect becomes the forefront of the battle to both promote individual autonomy and develop a truly public good. The intersubjective approach advocated by Dewey, while intending to be a democratic participatory form, becomes problematic by virtue of the fact that it ignores ideological production on the structural level. . . .Not only is intent thwarted but restraints on alternative perspectives have a chilling anti-democratic effect.[56]

The aim of this chapter has been to work out the philosophical details underlying the various claims that Dewey lacks a sufficient idea of power. The three lines of criticism developed here converge into a similar conclusion: Dewey's failure to recognize and duly consider manipulation and deceit as inherent factors within shared experience turns his idea of democracy into a pipe dream. The next chapter will measure the merits of these criticisms against the understanding of Dewey's work developed in this study up to this point. This analysis will make clear that Dewey was well aware of the effects of coercion and manipulation on individuals' habits and desires, all in the name of liberty, equality and cooperation. Therefore, in light of Dewey's idea of power, the next chapter will suggest that the democratic ideal becomes all the more urgent as the most intelligent, just, and enriching guide to social and political experience.

NOTES

[1] John Dewey and James Hayden Tufts, *Ethics,* 1908/1932; *John Dewey, The Later Works, 1925-1953,* vol. 7, edited by Jo Ann Boydston (Carbondale: Southern Illinois University Press, 1985): p. 228.

[2] Arthur O. Lovejoy, *The Thirteen Pragmatisms and Other Essays* (Baltimore: The Johns Hopkins Press, 1963): p. 150.

[3] See Chapter Two, "Background To Dewey's Thought: Realism and Idealism," pp. 9-13.

[4] Lovejoy, *The Thirteen Pragmatisms,* p. 188; see also pp. 140-144, 185-190.

[5] Lovejoy maintains that "if we apply the demand for temporalistic precision to this assumption, we are obliged to construe it as meaning that a thing is known at a given moment of cognition only if it is both existent and immediately experienced within the time-limits of that moment. But to demand in this sense that philosophy shall 'admit into its constructions only what is directly experienced' is to forbid philosophy to admit into its 'construction' of the knowledge-situation the things that are observably most characteristic of and indispensable to that situation, qua functional—and also qua social. For the moment of practical deliberation is concerned chiefly with things external to the direct experience of that moment" (*Thirteen Pragmatisms,* pp.188-189).

[6] Lovejoy, *Thirteen Pragmatisms,* pp. 26, 155-156.

[7] Lovejoy, *Thirteen* Pragmatisms, pp. 26-27.

[8] Lovejoy, *Thirteen Pragmatisms,* p .12. See also pp. 1-12, 16-29.

[9] Lovejoy, *Thirteen Pragmatisms,* pp. 149-169.

[10] Lovejoy, *Thirteen Pragmatisms,* p. 164. Lovejoy writes, "Mr. Dewey hereupon adds, it is true, that 'even in such cases the intellectual element is set in a context which is noncognitive.' But this. . .can scarcely mean more than that the raw material of human cognition consists of bare sensory data which might by themselves very well resemble the 'experience of the oyster or the growing bean vine.' Qua conscious and qua human, experience admittedly is—if not exclusively made up of—at least natively and constantly shot through with reflection; is irremediably addicted to the habit of taking present data as disclosures of the existence and nature of things other than themselves" (p. 164).

[11] Lovejoy, *Thirteen Pragmatisms,* pp. 16-17.

[12] Paul K. Crosser, *The Nihilism of John Dewey* (New York: Philosophical Library, Inc., 1955): p. x. See also pp. 3-72.

[13] Crosser, *The Nihilism of John Dewey,* p. 73.

[14] Crosser, *The Nihilism of John Dewey,* pp. ix-x.

[15] Russell Kirk, *The Conservative Mind: From Burke to Santayana* (Chicago: H. Regnery Co., 1953): pp. 7-9.

[16] Kirk, *The Conservative Mind,* p. 365.

[17] Kirk, *The Conservative Mind*, p. 9. See also pp. 365-366.

[18] C. Wright Mills, *Sociology and Pragmatism: The Higher Learning in America*, edited by Irving Louis Horowitz (New York: Paine-Whitman Publishers, 1964): p. 379. See also pp. 356-390.

[19] Mills, *Sociology and Pragmatism*, pp. 358-390. See especially pp. 358-361.

[20] See Chapter Two of this study, pp. 17-20.

[21] Mills, *Sociology and Pragmatism*, pp. 359-360.

[22] Mills, *Sociology and Pragmatism*, p. 358.

[23] Mills, *Sociology and Pragmatism*, pp. 358-362.

[24] Mills, *Sociology and Pragmatism*, pp. 360-361.

[25] Mills, *Sociology and Pragmatism*, pp. 375, 379. In essence, Mills is charging Dewey with carrying on the old empiricist foundation as explained in Chapter Two of this study, pp. 11-12.

[26] Mills, *Sociology and Pragmatism*, pp. 364-366, 385-387.

[27] Mills, *Sociology and Pragmatism*, p. 364.

[28] Mills, *Sociology and Pragmatism*, pp. 363, 376.

[29] Mills, *Sociology and Pragmatism*, p. 380.

[30] John Patrick Diggins, *The Promise of Pragmatism: Modernism and the Crisis of Knowledge and Authority* (Chicago and London: The University of Chicago Press, 1994).

[31] Diggins, *The Promise of Pragmatism*, p. 214. See pp. 212-249 for Diggins' analysis of Hegel's and Darwin's influence on Dewey.

[32] Diggins writes, "Drawing upon Darwin for a theory of nature, and on Hegel for an ontology that could absorb all dualisms, he developed a philosophical system that purported both to explain man's state of alienation and to offer a solution. . . .At the heart of Dewey's philosophy is his definition of man and nature. . . .Man was an 'organism' operating within a natural and social environment. A unified creature, man must be understood in biological terms, as a product of nature's evolutionary processes, and his problems must be seen as coterminous with those of nature. Man come into being, so to speak, when his mind begins to grope toward awareness and consciousness as a result of continuous interaction with a changing environment. From this process arises intelligence, the faculty that mediates between man and nature. The purpose of mind is to comprehend, adapt to, and eventually control an environment of change and flux" (*The Promise of Pragmatism*, p. 222). See also pp. 50-54; 158-249.

[33] Diggins, *The Promise of* Pragmatism, p. 227.

[34] Diggins, *The Promise of Pragmatism*, p. 223.

[35] Diggins, *The Promise of Pragmatism*, p. 226.

[36] Diggins, *The Promise of Pragmatism*, pp. 238-249.

[37] Diggins, *The Promise of Pragmatism*, p. 305.

[38] Diggins states that Dewey "happily accepted a definition of existence that depicted active man laboring to organize and control an unfinished and ever-evolving environment. Indeed man's continual need to 'readjust' to nature sparked the life of the mind that dramatized the height of human ingenuity. Yet Dewey's biological approach to human development prevented him from seeing also how the insecurities of existence result in the drive toward power as much as in the use of intelligence" (*The Promise of Pragmatism*, p. 224).

[39] Diggins, *The Promise of Pragmatism*, p. 228.

[40] Diggins, *The Promise of Pragmatism*, pp. 360-385; 386-426.

[41] Reinhold Niebuhr, *Christianity and Power Politics* (New York: Charles Scribner's Sons, 1946): p. 84.

[42] Reinhold Niebuhr, *Moral Man and Immoral Society: A Study in Ethics and Politics* (New York: Charles Scribner's Sons, 1932/1960): p. 35.

[43] Herbert Marcuse, "John Dewey's *Theory of Valuation,*" *John Dewey: Critical Assessments*, vol. III, edited by J. E. Tiles (London and New York: Routledge, 1992): pp. 22-27.

[44] Marcuse, "John Dewey's *Theory of Valuation,*" p. 25.

[45] John Ryder, "Community, Struggle, and Democracy: Marxism and Pragmatism,"*John Dewey: Critical Assessments*, vol. II, edited by J. E. Tiles (London and New York: Routledge, 1992): p. 348. Ryder suggests that "in the end, Dewey attributes the problems of a class divided society not to

fundamental differences in class interest, but to what he refers to as 'cultural lag,' and it is this move that generates the problem" (p. 347).

[46] Ryder, "Community, Struggle, and Democracy: Marxism and Pragmatism," p. 348.

[47] Marcuse, "John Dewey's *Theory of Valuation*," p. 25.

[48] Marcuse, "John Dewey's *Theory of Valuation*," p. 26.

[49] Joseph Flay, "Alienation and The Status Quo," *John Dewey: Critical Assessments*, vol. II, edited by J. E. Tiles (London and New York: Routledge, 1992): p. 309.

[50] Miguel Angel Estremera, *Democratic Theories of Hope: A Critical Comparative Analysis of The Public Philosophies of John Dewey and Henry A. Giroux* (Ph.D. dissertation, Rutgers The State University of New Jersey—New Brunswick, 1993).

[51] John Dewey, *Ethics, The Later Works*, vol. 7, pp. 224-225.

[52] Estremera, *Democratic Theories of Hope*, pp. 35-38.

[53] Flay, "Alienation and The Status Quo," p. 314.

[54] Flay, "Alienation and The Status Quo," p. 317.

[55] Estremera, *Democratic Theories of Hope*, p. 36.

[56] Estremera, *Democratic Theories of Hope*, p. 154.

A DEWEYAN RESPONSE

A brief summary of this study will provide the necessary framework for judging and responding to Dewey's critics' claims. This detail will make the point that Dewey was keenly aware of insidious power that rest upon hegemonic control of perspective. Furthermore, this analysis will make clear that Dewey understood this kind of power to have its most sophisticated and damaging effects when embodied through shared institutions, that is, the shared habits and practices that cultivate common feelings, thoughts, wants, and desires. Therefore, in light of Dewey's sense of power, this chapter will make the point that the practice of the democratic ideal serves as the most efficient and just means to combat every form of power that works to stunt individual and social growth. More specifically, this chapter will suggest, with Dewey, that the democratic ideal demands a relentless vigilance over the social conditions that influence shared habit and that nourish individual character. This watchful task entails the keen identification and measurement of social influences by individuals in their everyday struggles to judge and direct the course of their shared activities. As a moral ideal, democracy puts a premium on individual responsibility for making others responsible.

A BRIEF SUMMARY

As pointed out in Chapter Three, "The Roots of Dewey's Practical Philosophy," Dewey developed a keen awareness of the philosophical problems inherent in both the empiricist and rationalist traditions from the very outset of his professional career.[1] Through his mentor George S. Morris, Dewey came to see that British empiricism rested upon a metaphysical dualism between mind and matter that, in turn, resulted in a spiritual and moral skepticism. That is, Dewey understood the empiricist stance to hinge upon the idea that physical laws regulating physical matter also cause and regulate the human mind, a function of the brain, itself a physical substance. Dewey maintained that this metaphysical realism leaves the human mind as a mere passive by-product of the succession of pure matter. The empiricist epistemological problem, then, became one of having to explain how the phenomenon of mind can go beyond itself to account for physical phenomena as its supposed cause. "To say that the mind, if itself a mere phenomena or group of phenomena, can transcend phenomena and obtain knowledge of that reality which accounts both for other phenomena and for itself, is absurd."[2]

Dewey pointed out that in order for the empiricists to suggest that the mind is capable of such a feat presupposes a much more active conception of mental activity than the empiricist stance allows. It is in this sense that Dewey clearly understood the empiricist position to falter upon a mind and matter dualism.

Dewey suggested that a more accurate conception of mind consists of mental attention that maintains its integrity through successive feelings of phenomena and is capable of abstracting an idea of causal relation between these feelings. It is clear from Dewey's analysis of empiricism that his idea of human consciousness consists of both feeling caused by definite effects of phenomena and mental activity that retains and organizes this data into a continuous flow. However, Dewey did not blindly accept the traditional rationalist explanation for how the human mind organizes all sensory data into a meaningful flow of continuous experience.

Dewey understood Kant's transcendent realm of unconditioned meaning and Hegel's Absolute to result in a mind and matter dualism that reduces the human mind to a mere vessel for the workings of predetermined nonphenomena, the existence of which never can be verified by human sense. Therefore, according to Dewey, the rationalist metaphysical stance, particularly that argued by Kant and Hegel, lacks epistemological warrant. As pointed out in Chapter Three of this study, Dewey modified the rationalist metaphysical claim of absolute unity among all existence by use of the neurological findings from physiological psychology about the human organism. The result of this modification is a form of idealism that is consistent with Dewey's physio-psychologically informed assumptions about the epistemological and social nature of human experience and that avoids the dualism between mind and matter characteristic of both the empiricist and rationalist stances. More importantly, Dewey's reconstructed idealism provides a sound ethical justification for why all human capacities should be directed toward universal unity as their end.[3]

As pointed out in Chapter Four of this study, Dewey took "human consciousness" to mean the homogenous circuit of nervous activity by which the human being organizes its various sensory data and, by virtue of this capacity, is enabled to widen and enrich its response to the demands of circumstance. Dewey saw the human organism as one continuous conduction and reconstitution of nervous energy aimed at adjusting itself to its environment. He pointed to the apperceptive and retentive capacities of the human nervous system as the fundamental processes by which the human being coordinates its adjustment. Retention refers to the malleable capacity of the central nervous system to retain the effects of previous sensory-motor coordinations as these develop in response to contextual demands. As Dewey pointed out, retention serves as a digestive function of the nervous system that works in complementary fashion with the directive or ordering functions of apperception (association, dissociation, and attention). Together, these psycho-physiological processes make up the self-executing mechanism of habit.

Again, habit refers to the more or less defined line of sensory-motor discharge through which the human being not only physically adjusts to his or her environment but does so by associating, distinguishing, and attending to contextual qualities in relation to the particular line of activity. Thus, the meaning of sensory data develops in association with some particular line of activity (habit) such that the perception of this data comes to signify or call up an idea of the activity. That is, habit serves as the basis by which the individual connects and dissociates incoming sensory data according to the significance of the data in the realization of some on-going line of activity that defines the individual. Habits, then, are another way of indicating interests, or the active demands for those tendencies that define the self with special attention for the objects, feelings, and conditions necessary to bring these tendencies into effect. As the frequency and range of the individual's tendencies increase, his or her associative power increases because his or her means of connecting incoming data has expanded and become stronger. Thus the individual's perception of the significance of data becomes more refined, sensitive, and widened.[4]

A RESPONSE TO LOVEJOY, CROSSER, KIRK, MILLS, DIGGINS, AND MARCUSE

Dewey's epistemological stance entails a couple of things that suggest his critics are off the mark. A direct response to Arthur Lovejoy's criticism should be sufficient to stand as a general response to all of Dewey's critics, insofar as any of these critics charge him with metaphysical realism.

Lovejoy accuses Dewey of metaphysical and epistemological realism in which the meaning of the phenomenal world inheres in the phenomena themselves and is recognized in the mere sense of their immediate presence. It is true that in Dewey's account, the perception of some thing actually present to the senses is necessary for the recognition of meaning. However, as Dewey maintained, perception is that stage in apperception in which some felt quality is associated with a particular interest of the self and thus is given relation with an on-going activity. Therefore, upon Dewey's account, perception does not yield meaning inherent in things themselves but meaning insofar as the apparent qualities of phenomena are connected with the habits of the individual. Each successive stage in the recognition of meaning relies upon the increasing attention to the ways in which phenomena are connected with these activities. The perception of a quality amounts to immediate association with some interest, and this stimulates memory, a rushing forth of some past experience of the self such that the quality gains a temporal, continuous connection with a particular tendency to act. In turn, memory stimulates the forming of an idea about some particular activity.

This is what Dewey called conception, the focusing on a particular method or way of acting that is suggested by or called up through the perception of some stimulus. By connecting the immediate felt quality with some previously formed tendency to act, the individual begins to imagine and judge the future consequences if this method of acting is carried through. Thus, the individual estimates or judges an act more or less to be in harmony with the facts of the case before acting, carries out the act, and perceives the truth or harmony of his or her estimate as the consequences materialize. This is to suggest that the individual draws upon previous experience as a guide for future experience, the validity of which entails some degree of "ex post facto" measurement, insofar as the concrete meaning or significance of any proposition must wait to be borne out—or not—through the consequences of experience. Whatever cognitive indefiniteness in truth remains in

Dewey's account has to be attributed to the unpredictable contingencies of life itself.[5]

This summary, serves to reiterate the fact that Dewey adequately argued against any metaphysical stance suggesting that human conduct is determined and caused by some force (including Russell Kirk's "divine intent") existing outside of human experience. Dewey clearly portrayed human beings as being equipped with all the capacities of consciousness necessary to form their own response to environmental demands and to refine, strengthen, and expand this response according to their particular interests, contrary to what both Mills and Diggins suggest. As pointed out in Chapter Five, "Habit as Social Practice," Dewey fully recognized habit as an inherently social, acquired tendency to act. Other people cultivate and encourage certain tendencies in the individual that develop into active interests urging fulfillment or satisfaction. The individual acts and then enjoys or suffers the consequences, including—most importantly—the support, or withdrawal of it, by others. That is, others also instruct, correct, admonish, and demand that the individual control his or her desires so as to be considerate of and in harmony with the needs, expectations, and desires of those who share in the individual's conduct. The demands and expectations of others return to the individual and are retained more or less in association with the tendency, becoming part of its significance or meaning. This is to suggest, then, that the individual does not act simply for mere physical pleasure, as Kirk suggests, or according to a simple stimulus-response cycle, as Mills maintains. The habit or tendency is mediated more or less by the thought of the social consequences called up in association. The social consequences regulate the satisfaction of the impulse and give it a social definition and moral end.

According to Dewey, it is only through the acquisition and development of shared habits that the individual forms an idea about the end or good of his or her conduct and a standard by which to guide and measure its realization. In the most general sense, the cultivation of habit develops the idea that the good consists in the pursuit of individual desires as these are fulfilled through the objects and conditions that harmonize with the desires and growth of others. Insofar as the good includes the demands and expectations of others, the good always entails an idea of the right and wrong ways to satisfy one's desires. In this sense, the good also serves as the standard by which to guide and judge an idea of conduct beforehand and to measure its value in consequence after the fact. According to Dewey, shared habits enable individuals to realize a more perfect unity between their own happiness (individual liberty) and the happiness of others (social equality).[6]

> By personal choice among ends suggested by desires of objects which are in agreement with the needs of social relations, an individual achieves a kind of happiness which is harmonious with the happiness of others. This is the only sense in which there is an equation between personal and general happiness. But it is also the only sense which is morally required.[7]

Paul Crosser's insinuation that Dewey's philosophy leads to moral relativism simply cannot be sustained upon the claim that Dewey developed a simple subjectivist epistemology. It may be claimed, as Russell Kirk does, that Dewey undercuts the idea of theological or moral absolutes existing outside of all human experience but somehow working through and regulating it nonetheless. Kirk may mean that Dewey has left individuals with no cognitive ability to draw upon the significance of their previous experience as a guide for conduct. This charge would amount to "cognitive indeterminableness," to use Crosser's term, but, as pointed out above, it does not follow from a thorough analysis of Dewey's work. Perhaps Kirk means that Dewey has left individuals in fated struggles over the meaning of "harmony" and "happiness" with only their own devices to depend upon. That is, Dewey leaves social experience without any fixed, unconditioned principles to which every human being may appeal so as to adjudicate conflicting claims of right. In one respect, Kirk is correct. Dewey effectively argued that there is no epistemological warrant to prove the existence of metaphysical absolutes and suggested that such a metaphysical stance ultimately breaks apart into an insoluble mind and matter dualism. Therefore, Dewey saw the moral nature of human existence as metaphysically neutral, open, and subject to human determination and direction.

Contrary to what Mills and Diggins claim, Dewey maintained that human beings have all the powers of consciousness necessary to form and modify their responses in the environment, which includes all social relations as constituent parts. In keeping with this ontological foundation, Dewey's moral ideal is absolute in generic form but flexible in meaning. That is, the criterion suggests that the individual always act so as to bring about the fullest possible unity between his or her own happiness and the happiness of others. Stated another way, the criterion requires the individual always to do the best that he or she can. In this sense, the criterion is absolute. Of course, what this "best" means depends upon the circumstances of the case. The particular meaning of the criterion is relative to the individual's idea of the good as this includes the particular social demands and facts at hand.[8] A teacher's dictum that one never should let a moment of possible correction and instruction pass by may serve as the best idea under certain circumstances but might not be the best method to facilitate the open sharing of feelings about, for example, race in a public forum.

The criterion and its application both exist in terms of the individual's own moral life; it is always putting two and two together; doing the best possible with the material available. Its terms are the given impulse and its bearing in the agent's own life, it is simply a complete view, or judgment, of the intrinsic nature of the act. Only a criterion which does lie within the range of the self is workable; an outside criterion, just in the degree of its externality, will never translate into terms of the individual's own need and powers; it will not connect. . . .Such a criterion is absolute, yet relative. It is permanent, yet flexible. It is absolute in the sense of containing all its conditions and terms within itself, it is self as a living actuality. It is relative, in that it is not an abstract rule excluding all difference of circumstance, but applies to the concrete relations of the case. It is permanent or identical, because self is one in its life and movement; but flexible and variable since the self is one in and through activity and not by its mere static subsistence.[9]

Of course, as Kirk also points out, Dewey's ethical stance still leaves open the possibility of social conflict over claims of right. Dewey clearly recognized conflict and uncertainty as "ultimate traits" of human existence.[10] But, contrary to what Diggins claims, Dewey never argued or implied that the mere fact of social conflict by itself would effect a resolution of competing values outside of human study, imagination, and effort. And while Herbert Marcuse's claim that Dewey attributed social conflict to a maladjustment of values capable of repair by human reason is consistent with Dewey's ethical stance, Dewey never suggested that this repair is so simple as to believe that good faith in a just resolution naturally or automatically could prevail. He also was not so naïve to think that corruption will not influence the democratic process.

As pointed out in Chapter Five of the present study, Dewey understood social conflict to be generated by discrepancies between competing human interests and judgments as to the relative value of these interests. According to Dewey, the function and significance of conflict in human life is its sin qua non stimulation of detection and thought. "Conflict is the gadfly of thought. It stirs us to observation and memory. It instigates to invention. It shocks us out of sheep-like passivity, and sets us at noting and contriving. Not that it always effects this result."[11] This is to suggest that social conflict is an opportunity to recognize the facts at hand and to become clear about the sources of antagonism. However, again, Dewey had no illusions that individuals automatically will reach agreement when confronted by their differences or that all individuals necessarily will desire to do good instead of evil. To believe that human beings always will desire to act in good faith is to attribute to them an inherent ontological quality that not only lacks epistemological warrant but renders the environmental influences on human behavior irrelevant and reduces human misery and evil to exceptions of nature. Such an assumption contradicts every scientific and philosophical principle Dewey ever developed.

To reiterate, in light of his arguments against any and all metaphysical absolutes, Dewey consistently portrayed the moral nature of human beings as neutral and open, and therefore subject to human determination and direction for better or for worse. He did argue that consideration of the good and the right emerges organically from within shared practices and serves to guide individuals' desires and interests more or less. However, the idea that individuals will act in good faith is different from the idea that individuals should act in good faith.[12] Dewey argued that individuals should act in good faith to direct their affairs for the better. He maintained that a certain degree of faith in the good is necessary for the growth of interest in the first place. That is, since the growth of one's interests requires the nourishment and support of others, some degree of sympathy and consideration for and understanding of the needs of others is a prerequisite. To be good willed, to be motivated by and conscientious of the growth of oneself with due care and responsibility for the development of the capacities of others is a necessary virtue for self-realization. Thus, good faith refers to the belief that decency, honesty, wisdom, temperance, and courage towards others will lead to a freer and more equitable life together. Since individuals differ in the range and thoroughness of conscientiousness for others (the good), then good faith and good will always are matters of degree. Individuals exhibit it more or less.

In a sense, then, good will is another name for democratic disposition. It is an attitude that entails an ideal of justice to be realized as an ultimate end of conduct. Therefore, the ideal of good faith is one with the democratic ideal, which Dewey has argued is the most ethically justifiable end given the ontological nature of the individual as a self-determined, socially active creature. To confront social conflict democratically, in good faith, will not satisfy the ideal of justice automatically but will help pose the problem of justice more clearly.

> From the ethical point of view, therefore, it is not too much to say that the democratic ideal poses, rather than solves, the great problem: How to harmonize the development of each individual with the maintenance of a social state in which the activities of one will contribute to the good of all others. It expresses a postulate in the sense of a demand to be realized: That each individual shall have the opportunity for the release, expression, fulfillment, of his distinctive capacities, and that the outcome shall further the establishment of a fund of shared values. Like every true ideal, it signifies something to be done rather than something already given, something ready made. Because it is something to be accomplished by human planning and arrangement, it involves constant meeting and solving of problems—that is to say, the desired harmony never is brought about in a way which meets and forestalls all future developments. There is no shortcut to it, no single predestined road which can be found once for all and which, if human beings continue to walk in it without deviation, will surely conduct them to the good.[13]

To the claim that Dewey's philosophical assumptions undercut all moral standards by which to guide social conduct, the evidence suggests otherwise. According to Dewey, the heart of the democratic ideal is a just balance between individual liberty and social equality. As a moral standard, democratic justice poses the question, To what extent will the particular demands put forward actually contribute to a more meaningful idea of the good and increase the sense of responsibilities necessary to realize this good? In order to answer this question so that the significance of particular demands are filled out and a better, more meaningful course of conduct is made clear, a free and open exchange of perspectives guided by honesty and reason is necessary. Again, this is to restate that a democratic ideal necessitates a democratic method for its fulfillment.

A RESPONSE TO FLAY AND ESTREMERA

Joseph Flay and Miguel Estremera doubt that Dewey's version of the democratic method can deliver the goods. According to Flay and Estremera, Dewey's failure to account for the influence of manipulation and deceit on the democratic process leaves his argument for free and open discussion as the means to secure a greater justice and freedom so simplistic that it allows powerful ill-will to conceal itself behind the cloak of the "social good." By virtue of this failure, Dewey did not conceive of power as the control over people's needs, desires, wants, and ways of judgment. In turn, Dewey did not see how individuals come to identify with and struggle for values antithetical to their own growth and legitimize their own subjugation as natural. To put it in more current terms, Dewey failed to account for a sophisticated and efficient form of power that rests upon the hegemonic control of perspective and that manufactures a "false consciousness" that precludes the realization of an authentic democratic society.

Flay's and Estremera's claim amounts to the idea that Dewey did not recognize individuals' power to affect shared living conditions in such a way as to influence the development of shared habits. As pointed out in Chapters Four and Five, Dewey's entire philosophy is predicated upon the fact that the human organism is thoroughly saturated by its environment, which is always social. Every one of the organism's effective capacities (habits) is nourished and cultivated by means of its social environment.

> The agent is moulded through education, unconscious and conscious, into certain habits of thinking and feeling as well as acting. His acts, therefore, partake of the aims and disposition of his race and time. . . .Our acts are controlled by the demands made upon us. These demands include not simply the express requirements of other persons, but the customary expectations of the family, social circle, trade or profession; the stimuli of surrounding objects, tools, books, etc.; the range and quality of opportunities afforded.[14]

In short, the social environment affects the growth of the individual and the individual affects the social environment, all for better or worse. Dewey's recognition of this fact alone provides enough evidence to suggest that he was well aware that individuals _may_ affect patterns of thought and desire by way of affecting shared conditions and practices. "Social institutions, the trend of occupations, the pattern of social arrangements, are the finally controlling influences in shaping minds."[15] Now, did Dewey recognize that individuals or groups may control social institutions for private profit? A cursory search through what are considered Dewey's more political works uncovers ample evidence to support the judgment that he was keenly aware of this possibility.[16]

Dewey clearly recognized subtle sleight of hand and outright deception as parts of the workings of power over others. In Ethics, for example, he suggested that "adulteration of intellectual material is as harmful socially as adulteration of foods is physiologically. Secrecy and falsification are the chief enemies which democratic ideals have to contend with."[17] More, as he writes in a 1937 article entitled "Freedom," "The forces which work to undermine freedom appear in even subtler form as society grows more complex and operate more insidiously. They are more effective just because in their first appearance they do not seem to be oppressive to liberty. Indeed, in the first appearance and early stages of operation, they are likely to be welcomed for some obvious advantages they bring with them—possibly even a promise of greater freedom."[18] Furthermore, Dewey clearly recognized that the most efficient form of power is control over emotional and intellectual habits. In *The Public and Its Problems*, Dewey suggests that "the smoothest road to control of political conduct is by control of opinion."[19]

> It would be a mistake to identify the conditions which limit free communication and circulation of facts and ideas, and which thereby arrest and pervert social thought or inquiry, merely with overt forces which are obstructive. It is true that those who have the ability to manipulate social relations for their own advantage have to be reckoned with. They have an uncanny instinct for detecting whatever intellectual tendencies even remotely threaten to encroach upon their control. They have developed an extraordinary facility in enlisting upon their side the inertia, prejudices and emotional partisanship of the masses by use of a technique which impedes free inquiry and expression. We seem to be approaching a state of government by hired promoters of opinion called publicity agents. But the more serious enemy is deeply concealed in hidden entrenchments. . . .Emotional habituations and intellectual habitudes on the part of the mass of men create the conditions of which the exploiters of sentiment and opinion only take advantage.[20]

Estremera, however, suggests that while Dewey acknowledged the existence of those who take advantage of the emotional and intellectual habits of others, he did not fully account for the fact that these same individuals generate or create subjugating habits in others in the first place. There is, however, plenty of evidence in Dewey's work to suggest otherwise.

> A still greater invasion of freedom of thought comes about by subtler and more insidious means. Just because public opinion and sentiment are so powerful in a democratic country, even when its democracy is largely nominal, it is immensely worth while for any group which wishes to control public action to regulate their formation. This is best done at their source— while, that is, they are still in process of forming. Propaganda is the method used. Hence we have today a multitude of agencies which skillfully manipulate and color the news and information, which circulate, and which artfully instill, under the guise of disinterested publicity, ideas favorable to hidden interests. The public press, which reaches almost every individual and which circulates cheaply and rapidly, affords an organ of unprecedented power for accomplishing a perversion of public opinion. Favorable and unfavorable presentation of individuals, laudation and ridicule, subtle suggestion of points of view, deliberate falsification of facts and deliberate invention of half-truth or whole falsities, inculcate by methods, of which those subject to them are not even aware, the particular tenets which are needed to support private and covert policies.[21]

LAISSEZ-FAIRE CAPITALISM: AN EXAMPLE OF HEGEMONY

Dewey not only recognized the threat of overt force and the manufacture of desire as fundamental pillars of power but often took the complex relations of capitalism as a convenient example to explore this point. The sophistication of Dewey's understanding of power lies in the detail of this example.

Throughout his political works, Dewey suggests that the same forces that have made democratic forms of self-government possible also have served as the means by which laissez-faire capitalism flourishes. In *Liberalism and Social Action*, Dewey argues that while the concern about the essence of and proper relation between the individual, freedom, and the universal may be traced back to Greek thought, the modern formulation of this relation developed out of the empiricist-rationalist traditions, particularly out of the work of John Locke.[22] Since the early Enlightenment, philosophers had been struggling to establish the idea that human beings are held together both physically and spiritually by constant laws permeating the universe. Philosophers from both the empiricist and rationalist traditions argued that each individual has the capacity to sense and understand the laws of nature for himself. Through test, intelligence, and effort, individuals could induce the constant truths of the universe and therefore enlighten themselves. This self-enlightenment, in turn, would lead to a freer and more just society, a society in which individuals forge a self-government in keeping with the universal law. According to Dewey, by the late 1600s, Locke had worked out a set of moral and political implications from these metaphysical and epistemological tenets.

Locke maintained, according to Dewey, that individuals have a right to seek and understand the universal laws for themselves, a right not bestowed upon them by any social organization but granted to them by nature itself. Furthermore, Locke suggested that it is a duty for individuals to conduct themselves according to their understanding of the natural laws and, in turn, to forge a contract of collective regulation with others as they come to understand the natural laws for themselves. This duty rests upon the belief that individuals are the best judges not only of their own interests but of the best means necessary to bring these interests to fruition. According to the natural abilities and diligence of the individual in discovering his interests, the resulting industry and effort of each individual (the part) would contribute to the social good (the whole). Therefore, Locke argued, the individual must remain free of physical and intellectual coercion of all kinds, including binding tradition and corrupt authority, in order to help realize a better society and thus a more complete universe. Government, then, would not be an imposed or coerced arrangement but a contract of mutual consent entered into by the aggregate of individuals who are assumably free to be clear about their personal interests beforehand. According to Dewey, democracy, both as a way of living together and as a form of self-government, grew out of the faith in the dignity and natural right of individuals to realize freely the truths of the universe for themselves.

As Dewey points out, however, it followed from the tenet of the free individual that people have a natural right to the fruits of their labor, that is, a natural right to acquire property and profit. Without this right legally secured, the individual would be discouraged to exert energy toward an end that could be taken away, and, thus, social progress, which depends upon human industry, would suffer. Therefore, the natural right to own property required full protection from infringement and seizure. Since the tenet of the free individual entailed the dignity to determine one's own interest, any contractual relationship that the individual entered into was assumed to be done out of free choice and with the responsibility for understanding the conditions and consequences of such arrangements. Thus, contracts between individuals necessitated enforcement since they are a means to secure private property. The function of self-government, therefore, was to ensure that individuals remain free and non-obstructed in pursuit of their own interest.

> Economic "laws," that of labor springing from natural wants and leading to the creation of wealth, of present abstinence in behalf of future enjoyment leading to creation of capital effective in piling up still more wealth, the free play of competitive exchange, designated the law of supply and demand, were "natural" laws. They were set in opposition to political laws as artificial, man-made affairs. The inherited tradition which remained least questioned was a conception of Nature which made Nature something to conjure with. The older metaphysical conception of Natural Law was, however, changed into an economic conception; laws of nature, implanted in human nature, regulated the production and exchange of goods and services, and in such a way that when they were kept free from artificial, that is political, meddling, they resulted in the maximum possible social prosperity and progress. . . .The economic theory of laissez-faire, based upon belief in beneficent natural laws which brought about harmony of personal profit and social benefit, was readily fused with the doctrine of natural rights. . . .Each person naturally seeks the betterment of his own lot. This can be attained only by industry. Each person is naturally the best judge of his own interests, and if left free from the influence of artificially imposed restrictions, will express his judgment in his choice of work and exchange of services and goods. Thus, barring accident, he will contribute to his own happiness in the measure of his energy in work, his shrewdness in exchange and his self-denying thrift. Wealth and security are the natural rewards of economic virtues. . . .Under the invisible hand of a beneficent providence which has framed natural laws, work, capital and trade operate harmoniously to the advantage and advance of men collectively and individually. The foe to be dreaded is interference of government. Political regulation is needed only because individuals accidentally and purposely—since the possession of property by the industrious and able is a temptation to the idle and shiftless—encroach upon one another's activities and properties. This encroachment is the essence of injustice, and the function of government is to secure justice—which signifies chiefly the protection of property and of contracts which attend commercial exchange.[23]

According to Dewey, what the Enlightenment philosophers offered to early capitalist arrangements was a gritty account of man and matter and a reasoned

107

excuse for the accumulation of private property as a natural inclination, right, and duty.[24] Dewey maintains that insofar as individual liberty and social progress were interpreted and identified strictly with the growth of economic liberty, as opposed to social and political liberty, then the Enlightenment principle of individual freedom sanctified the relations of capitalism such that its end became a shared moral compulsion. As Dewey suggests in *Ethics,* this compulsion rests upon "the notion that individuals left free to pursue their own advantage in industry and trade will not only best further their own private interests but will also best promote social progress and contribute most effectively to the satisfaction of the needs of others and hence to the general happiness."[25] According to Dewey, the social claim was and is made that the relations of capitalism rest upon the natural right to industry and profit and that this natural right is essential to the objective realization of the universal law and social good. This claim entails the idea that the objective realization of the universal law directly depends upon the degree to which individuals bring their intelligence, industry, thrift, and tenacity to bear. Since the realization of the universal law is not complete as of yet, the only true measure of its present realization is in terms of the resources or wealth generated by industry and thrift. Therefore, the production and accumulation of wealth is claimed as a moral duty commanded by universal law.[26]

As Dewey suggests in *Liberalism and Social Action,* "When it became evident that disparity, not equality, was the actual consequence of laissez faire liberalism, defenders of the latter developed a double system of justifying apologetics."[27] Dewey points out that appeal to the natural inequalities of individuals is used not only to account for the existence of exorbitant wealth along side heaping poverty but to justify this disparity as the fair workings of nature. That is, since it is a fact that individuals manifest various degrees of intellectual and physical abilities, the differences between wealth and poverty are claimed to be direct results of the differences in these natural abilities. As the argument runs, the laws of conflict and struggle inherent in nature expose those with the superior balance of intelligence and strength, who naturally emerge as the public stewards for those who are less able. Thus, the differences in social and political power are justified as natural.

Dewey suggests that to complete this justification, an appeal is made that the realization of a larger social good lies within each individual's capacity to be more self-reliant, judicious, industrious, and intelligent.[28] The appeal comes with the promise that exhibiting and intensifying these virtues will create the opportunity for personal and social improvement. In keeping with the atomistic tenets of the Enlightenment philosophy, the appeal entails the assumption that each individual, regardless of circumstance, is equally free to judge, choose, and execute what is in his or her best interest, insofar as his or her interest is consistent with the universal law. For example, as Dewey describes the matter, "In legal theory, the individual who has a starving family to support is equal in making a bargain about hours and conditions of labor and wages, with an employer who has large accumulated wealth to fall back on, and who finds that many other workers near the subsistence line are clamoring for an opportunity to earn something with which to support their families."[29] The outcome or degree of success, however, is claimed to be directly dependent upon natural capacities and effort. As Dewey points out, the appeal entails extortion through fear. Those entrenched with great economic power make the claim that any disturbance of existing economic conditions will undermine both the just order of nature and the further realization of personal welfare and the public good. "Their use of power to maintain their own interests is met, from the other side, by widespread fear of any disturbance, lest it be for the worse. This fear of any change is greatly enhanced by the complexity of the existing social scheme, where a change at one point may spread in unforeseen ways and perhaps put all established values in peril. Thus an active and powerful self-interest in maintaining the status quo conspires with dread. . .to identify loyal citizenship with mental acquiescence in and blind laudation of things as they are."[30]

To state it simply, Dewey acknowledged the threat of overt force and implicit coercion as forms of power over others. In various places, he suggested that the interpretation and justification of the atomistic individual as the backbone of democratic liberty provides the sanction for governmental force against striking workers who supposedly violate their employment contracts, interfere with the capitalist claims to profit, and hence impede the so-called social good. He also understood that the ability to administer rewards and punishments in consequence of actions in support and protest of capitalist relations enable those invested with great economic power to command attention to their demands as social claims of right. Now, Dewey's recognition of physical threat and implicit coercion as means to command attention, coupled with his understanding of the influence of the social environment on the development of impulse and habit, provides a response to Estremera's claim that Dewey's idea of power lacks sophistication.

> The social medium neither implants certain desires and ideas directly, nor yet merely establishes certain purely muscular habits of action. . . .Setting up conditions which stimulate certain visible and tangible ways of acting is the first step. Making the individual a sharer or partner in the associated activity so that he feels its success as his success, its failure as his failure, is the completing step. As soon as he is possessed by the emotional attitude of the group, he will be alert to recognize the special ends at which it aims and the means employed to secure success. His beliefs and ideas, in other words, will take a form similar to those of others in the group.[31]

In light of the above quotation and in light of Dewey's understanding of the ethical nature of human conduct, it follows Dewey understood that power can be as productive and oppressive as it can be productive and liberating. This idea requires a brief explanation.

As developed in Chapter Five of the present study, Dewey well understood the mechanism of habit to be the basis for the psychological and social development of moral conduct.[32] He maintained that habit consists of a train of associated impulses, accumulated and modified over time according to the quality of consequences produced in the social environment and retained by the individual. The stimulation of one impulse calls up the train of others such that those called up check, inhibit, direct, and stimulate its further expression. That is, the associated impulses give relation and significance to the inducing impulse: they serve as the standard for its measurement (the right) and constitute its good. Again, as Dewey puts it, "In this aspect, they are the law, the controlling power of that impulse. They determine in what form, under what conditions of time, place and quality, it may be satisfied. Thus they determine or measure its value."[33]

Dewey recognized that by means of deception, promise of reward, threat of physical harm, and coercion, powerful ill-willed individuals may influence the particular conditions that feed shared habits and therefore, in various degrees, command impulse, need, want, and desire. For example, insofar as the ends and means serving selfish gain become a—if not the—mediating law of shared habit, then this end becomes the standard of measurement regulating all associated impulses and emotions, working to inhibit, stimulate, or reinforce their expression. That is, to the degree that the idea of unregulated profit proclaimed as a natural right and good sets up into the living fiber of shared habits, then individuals more or less will conduct themselves towards this end and legitimize the consequences as the inevitable and just outcome of nature. In direct response to Estremera's claim, Dewey was well aware that powerful individuals can affect and have affected social institutions through which others form and judge ends of conduct. Put differently, Dewey recognized the ability of powerful ill will to influence the formation of character and thus to affect the way and extent to which individuals judge the relations of power that affect them.

> When tradition and social custom are incorporated in the working constitution of an individual, they have authority as a matter of course over his beliefs and his activities. The forces that exert and exercise this authority are so much and so deep a part of individuals that there is no thought or feeling of their being external and oppressive. They cannot be regarded as hostile to individuals as long as they are built into the habitual beliefs and purposes of the individual. They support him and give him direction. They naturally compel his allegiance and arouse his devotion. Attack upon the authoritative institutions in which custom and tradition are embodied is, therefore, naturally resented by the individual; it is deeply resented as an attack upon what is deepest and truest in himself.[34]

Contrary to what his critics claim, the evidence from Dewey's work is clear: Dewey recognized that democracy provides an ethical shield for two-faced human conduct. He recognized that, on the one hand, the chief tenets of the democratic faith (individual dignity, universal law, and progress) contain the possibility to free human conduct from all sorts of socio-political tyranny. He also saw that, on the other hand, these same democratic principles contain the possibility to free human conduct to produce shackling, detrimental effects justified on the basis of the same universal law and aimed at the supposedly same common good. Now, Is Dewey's idea of the democratic method a sufficient means to combat the insidious forms of power that pervert the democratic ideal?

"DEMOCRATIC ENDS DEMAND DEMOCRATIC METHODS"

As pointed out at the end of Chapter Five of this study, the democratic ideal (individual liberty and social equality) emerges out of the faith in the individual to define and develop her particular capacities in harmony with the needs and demands of others as they define and develop their own powers.[35] As the good of conduct, the democratic ideal refers to the individual's conscious tendencies to grow in a way that is considerate, sympathetic, and enriching towards those who share in the consequences of his or her actions. As a standard of judgment, the ideal refers to the degree to which happiness and harmony are brought about in actual effect of acting upon his or her idea of the good. It follows, then, that the individual has the right and duty to act with a common good in mind. And, as new potentials are realized, new consequences, demands, and claims of right emerge that require a recalibration of action and a broader idea of a common good. Dewey has pointed out that the democratic ideal poses rather than solves the constant problem of achieving the right balance between individual freedom and social equality—justice, in a word. As Dewey puts it, "Both historically and actually the possibility of realization of the democratic ideal is conditioned, therefore, upon the possibility of working out in social practice and social institutions a combination of equality and liberty. . . .The problem is a practical one."[36]

That the democratic problem is a practical one suggests that it gets its concrete form and meaning from within the various associations that individuals share with each other. Therefore, the particular meaning of liberty, equality, justice, and hence power are determined by individuals as they define and measure the particular consequences of acting for some specific good upon the growth of their individual capacities and upon the shared conditions that nourish this growth. For example, as Dewey puts it in *Liberalism and Social Action*, "Liberty in the concrete signifies release from the impact of particular oppressive forces. . . .The direct impact of liberty always has to do with some class or group that is suffering in a special way from some form of constraint exercised by the distribution of powers that exists."[37]

This is to say that democracy in general can be realized only to the degree that individuals put it into practice through the particular shared activities that define them and give them purpose. A more just and enriching relation between the development of one's potential and that of all others can be established, refined, and expanded only to the extent that individuals strive to be thoughtful, appreciative, and understanding of each other in everything they do. As Dewey suggests, democracy is a way of acting, "a personal way of individual life," a certain way of forming and measuring the ends of conduct. It is, Dewey says, "the continual use of certain attitudes" characterized by the belief that others serve as vital resources and guides and that the incipient possibilities of human life are best sought for and realized through mutual reference and pooled intelligence. Furthermore, commitment to the democratic way of life entails certain rights and obligations necessary for embodying its animating principles. To draw upon others as resources, to be respectful and enriching to them requires open communication, free expression, and intimate exchange of perspective.

> The idea of democracy as opposed to any conception of aristocracy is that every individual must be consulted in such a way, actively not passively, that he himself becomes a part of the process of authority, of the process of social control; that his needs and wants have a chance to be registered in a way where they count in determining social policy. Along with that goes, of course, the other feature which is necessary for the realization of democracy—mutual conference and mutual consultation and arriving ultimately at social control by pooling, by putting together all of these individual expressions of ideas and wants.[38]

In other words, free expression is vital for individuals to define and realize the growth of their capacities and interests. The give and take of ideas provides the crucial means by which individuals alert each other about the enhancing or debilitating effects of their actions upon the shared conditions that nurture each of them. Since the problem of democracy is the development of the liberties of one so as to enrich the liberties of all, adequate knowledge of actual conditions and existing relations is put at a premium. Open discussion multiplies the possible range and thoroughness of perspective and judgment and, thus, allows for sharper consideration of new demands and claims that induce to a broader conception of democratic justice.

According to Dewey, "To cooperate by giving differences a chance to show themselves because of the belief that expression of difference is not only a right of other persons but is a means of enriching one's own life-experience, is inherent in the democratic personal way of life."[39] Dewey rightfully argues, therefore, that any other means would violate the democratic principles. He says that "recourse to monistic, wholesale, absolutist procedures is a betrayal of human freedom no matter in what guise it presents itself."[40] The use of violence and force, for example, to expedite the realization of democratic ideals ultimately imposes upon the right of individuals to define and develop their own interests as they see fit. The censorship and suppression of ideas ostensibly conducted for the preservation of freedom and equality violates the individual's right to contribute to the formation of values in which all share. The blind appeal and justification of "things as they are," glorified as time-tested routine, eventually turns the best of tradition into dogmatic principle that, in turn, necessarily shuts out differences in perspective and denies to those who suffer the right to be heard and taken seriously. As Dewey maintains, the alternatives to democratic authority condemn individuals to a life that is neither good nor common.[41]

> For what is the faith of democracy in the role of consultation, of conference, of persuasion, of discussion, in formation of public opinion, which in the long run is self-corrective, except faith in the capacity of the intelligence of the common man to respond with commonsense to the free play of facts and ideas which are secured by effective guarantees of free inquiry, free assembly and free communication? I am willing to leave to upholders of totalitarian

states of the right and the left the view that faith in the capacities of intelligence is utopian. For the faith is so deeply embedded in the methods which are intrinsic to democracy that when a professed democrat denies the faith he convicts himself of treachery to his profession.[42]

Dewey points out that the right to develop intelligence also entails the civic duty to use it to protect, discover, and enhance the conditions that nourish more democratic associations with others. This duty entails constant watchfulness over existing conditions and relations that one is a part of. As Dewey says in *Freedom and Culture*, "The struggle for democracy has to be maintained on as many fronts as culture has aspects: political, economic, international, educational, scientific and artistic, religious."[43] A commitment to democracy requires that each individual bring his or her best at detecting and exposing inequalities that stunt the growth of shared habits and block the development of more sensitive communication with each other. Even though democratic freedom allows any claim to be put forward, it does not follow that the claim automatically will be in harmony with what others take to be the good or that it will produce good in fact. Since the test of any social arrangement set up in the name of democracy is measured according to the concrete effects on habits, thoughts, purposes, and conditions, then it is a civic duty to test, reflect upon, and judge critically the degree to which social arrangements produce freedom and equality in people's lives. It follows that professed interest in democratic justice is measured in terms of the actual consequences produced in deed.

As Dewey puts the matter, "If a man says he is interested in pictures, he asserts that he cares for them; if he does not go near them, if he takes no pains to create opportunities for viewing and studying them, his actions so belie his words that we know this interest is merely nominal. Interest is regard, concern, solicitude for an object; if it is not manifested in action it is unreal."[44] Thus, the burden of proof is upon those individuals or groups who proclaim to act in the name of liberty and justice but who produce consequences serving selfish gain and setting up conditions that narrow individuals' effective choice and judgment. To be motivated by democratic ideals and to produce consequences antithetical to them is one thing; all human beings are capable of error and correction. But to persist in proclaiming interest for freedom and justice with knowledge that effects are otherwise constitutes faithlessness to democracy. "Wrong consists in faithlessness to that upon which the wrong doer counts when he is judging and seeking for what is good to him. He betrays the principles upon which he depends; he turns to his personal advantage the very values which he refuses to acknowledge in his own conduct towards others."[45] Therefore, democratic freedom implies a moral obligation to maintain an ever refined vigilance for each other, to inform others of their efforts and to direct them to broaden their idea of the democratic good by alerting them to new social demands to which they should hold themselves accountable. In this sense, the essence of democratic responsibility is making sure others develop a sense of democratic responsibility. Dewey is suggestive of the spirit of this duty in *Ethics*.

Responsibility in relation to control of our reactions to the conduct of others is twofold. The persons who employ praise and blame, reward and punishment, are responsible for the selection of those methods which will, with the greatest probability, modify in a desirable way the future attitude and conduct of others. There is no inherent principle of retributive justice that commands and justifies the use of reward and punishment independent of their consequences in each specific case. . . .One is held responsible in order that he may become responsible, that is, responsive to the needs and claims of others, to the obligations implicit in his position. Those who hold others accountable for their conduct are themselves accountable for doing it in such a manner that this responsiveness develops. Otherwise they are themselves irresponsible in their own conduct."[46]

In light of Dewey's understanding that power may take subtle and insidious forms, is his idea of the democratic method sufficient to fight this type of power? With Dewey, the answer rests in individuals' willingness to draw upon each other in increasingly complex and intimate ways to serve as lookouts for detrimental arrangements and as resources for reexamining and revising existing social practices. That is, the authority and power of the democratic method lies in individuals' incessant efforts at critical distinction and acute judgment of manipulative relations and their ingenuity for gathering and linking various forms of collective pressure in support or protest. However, Dewey was not blind to the enormity of the task. He maintained that "at the end as at the beginning the democratic method is as fundamentally simple and as immensely difficult as is the energetic, unflagging, unceasing creation of an ever-present new road upon which we can walk together."[47] But, despite the Sisyphean nature of the task, Dewey maintained a great faith in the power of human courage, effort, and—most of all—intelligence to make experience better and fuller. He also provided every sound philosophical reason for believing so. Is it naïve to believe that human beings have all the capacities necessary to correct themselves, to force, through peaceful discussion and collective pressure, entrenched forms of power to act for a greater justice? Dewey answers: "Is human nature intrinsically such a poor thing that the idea is absurd? I do not attempt to give any answer, but the word faith is intentionally used. For in the long run democracy will stand or fall with the possibility of maintaining the faith and justifying it by works."[48]

Is the civic responsibility to watch after and direct each other by way of open expression, meeting, mutual exchange, and collective judgment sufficient to detect and correct the ideas and habits of thought by which those subjugated legitimize their own subjugation? As Dewey points out, freedom cannot be forced on or handed to anyone. Furthermore, freedom is not simply a matter of relieving others from external constraint.[49] The cultivation of freedom (that is, effective power) in others requires the fostering of certain ways of acting, ways of critically forming and judging ends by reference to consequences on the growth of shared interests, and ways of choosing and ordering the realization of these consequences such that activity appreciates in meaning—in a word, education. According to Dewey, effective capacity—power—has to be built up through voluntary cooperation with each other in shared activities kindled by emotion and guided by intimate communication. As Dewey points out in a number of ways, communication is education in its widest sense. Since the vital nerve of extending the meaning and range of democratic freedom and equality is communication, it follows that education, in its formal institutional sense, is the nurse of democracy. Therefore, the problem of democratic justice is the problem of a democratic education.[50]

NOTES

[1] See pp. 24-35 of this study. See especially pp. 24-28 for an explication of Dewey's analysis of empiricism and pp. 28-35 for an explication of Dewey's reconstruction of his rationalist roots.

[2] John Dewey, "The Metaphysical Assumptions of Materialism," *John Dewey, The Early Works, 1882-1898*, vol. 1, edited by Jo Ann Boydston (Carbondale: Southern Illinois University Press, 1969): p. 6.

[3] For the particular metaphysical and epistemological problems that the rationalist tradition posed for Dewey, as well as Dewey's solutions to these problems, see Chapter Three, "The Roots of Dewey's Practical Philosophy," pp. 28-29 of this study.

[4] See Chapter Four, "Habit: The Seat of Dewey's Idea of Power," pp. 39-51. See especially pp. 40-46 for Dewey's idea of apperception and retention as the foundation of habit.

[5] See Chapter Four, particularly pp. 40-42.

[6] See Chapter Five, "Habit as Social Practice: A Means for Judging Power," pp. 52-70.

[7] John Dewey and James Hayden Tufts, *Ethics*, (1908/1932), *John Dewey, The Later Works, 1925-1953*, vol. 7, edited by Jo Ann Boydston (Carbondale: Southern Illinois University Press, 1985): p. 248.

[8] John Dewey, *The Study of Ethics: A Syllabus*, (1894), *John Dewey, The Early Works, 1882-1898*, vol. 4, edited by Jo Ann Boydston (Carbondale: Southern Illinois University Press, 1971): pp. 289-290.

[9] Dewey, *The Study of Ethics: A Syllabus, The Early Works*, vol. 4, p. 289.

[10] John Dewey, *Human Nature and Conduct: An Introduction to Social Psychology* (New York: The Modern Library, 1922): p. 12. See also John Dewey, *Experience and Nature* (New York: Dover Publications, INC., 1958).

[11] Dewey, *Human Nature and Conduct*, p. 300.

[12] John Dewey, *Freedom and Culture*, (1939), *John Dewey, The Later Works, 1925-1953*, vol. 13, edited by Jo Ann Boydston (Carbondale: Southern Illinois University Press, 1988): pp. 150-153. Dewey points out that "we cannot continue the idea that human nature when left to itself, when freed from external arbitrary restrictions, will tend to the production of democratic institutions that work successfully. We have now to state the issue from the other side. We have to see that democracy means the belief that humanistic culture *should* prevail; we should be frank and open in our recognition that the proposition is a moral one—like any idea that concerns what *should* be" (p. 151).

[13] Dewey, *Ethics, The Later Works*, vol. 7, p. 350.

[14] Dewey, *The Study of Ethics: A Syllabus, The Early Works*, vol. 4, p. 229.

[15] John Dewey, *Individualism, Old and New*, (1929), *John Dewey, The Later Works, 1925-1953*, vol. 5, pp. 102, edited by Jo Ann Boydston (Carbondale: Southern Illinois University Press, 1984): p. 102. The evidence that Dewey was aware of and understood the need to combat powerful influence shaping social institutions is clear and many. For example, Dewey writes, "It is indeed necessary to have freedom of thought and expression. But just because this is necessary for the health and progress of society, it is even more necessary that ideas should be genuine ideas, not sham ones, the fruit of inquiry, of observation and experimentation, the collection and weighing of evidence. The formation of the attitudes which move steadily in this direction is the work and responsibility of the school more than any other single institution. Routine and formal instruction, undemocratic administration of schools, is perhaps the surest way of creating a human product that submits readily

to external authority, whether that be imposed by force or by custom and tradition, or by the various forms of social pressure which the existing economic system produces" ("Freedom," *John Dewey, The Later Works, 1925-1953*, vol. 11, edited by Jo Ann Boydston (Carbondale: Southern Illinois University Press, 1987): pp. 253-254).

[16] See Chapter Five, n. 25, p.70.

[17] Dewey, *Ethics, The Later Works*, vol. 7, p. 359.

[18] John Dewey, "Freedom," *The Later Works*, vol. 11, p.247.

[19] John Dewey, *The Public and Its Problems* (Chicago: The Swallow Press, 1927): p. 182.

[20] Dewey, *The Public and Its Problems*, p. 169.

[21] Dewey, *Ethics, The Later Works*, vol. 7, pp. 360-361.

[22] John Dewey, *Liberalism and Social Action* (1935), *John Dewey, The Later Works, 1925-1953*, vol. 11, edited by Jo Ann Boydston (Carbondale: Southern Illinois University Press, 1987): p. 6-9. For Dewey's understanding of the philosophical and historical development of democratic forms of self-government in relation to the development of laissez faire capitalism, see all of *Liberalism and Social Action*; *Freedom and Culture, The Later Works*, vol. 13, pp. 136-155; *The Public and Its Problems*, pp. 75-109; and "The Future of Liberalism," *The Later Works*, vol. 11, pp. 289-295.

[23] Dewey, *The Public and Its Problems*, pp. 90-92.

[24] Dewey, *Liberalism and Social Action, The Later Works*, vol. 11, pp. 5-22; *Ethics, The Later Works*, vol. 7, pp. 331-339. In "Authority and Social Change," Dewey writes, "The new economic forces also claimed the right to supreme authority on the ground that they were pure and literal expressions of natural law—in contradistinction to political laws and institutions which, in so far as they did not conform to the play of economic forces, were artificial and man-made. Economic forces, through their representatives, interpreters and agents—the official economists and industrialists—claimed the divine prerogative to reign supreme over all human terrestrial affairs. The economist and industrialist and financier were the new pretenders to the old divine right of kings" (*The Later Works*, vol. 11, p. 135).

[25] Dewey, *Ethics, The Later Works*, vol. 7, p. 331.

[26] See *Ethics, The Later Works*, vol. 7, pp. 331-333; *The Public and Its Problems*, pp. 90-92.

[27] Dewey, *Liberalism and Social Action, The Later Works*, vol. 11, p. 29. See also "Authority and Social Change," *The Later Works*, vol. 11, pp. 136-137; "The Future of Liberalism," *The Later Works*, vol. 11, 289-295.

[28] Dewey, *Liberalism and Social Action, The Later Works*, vol. 11, pp. 29-30. As Dewey is well aware, "Even when words remain the same, they mean something very different when they are uttered by a minority struggling against repressive measures, and when expressed by a group that has attained power and then uses ideas that were once weapons of emancipation as instruments for keeping the power and wealth they have obtained. Ideas that at one time are means of producing social change have not the same meaning when they are used as means of preventing social change. This fact is itself an illustration of historic relativity, and an evidence of the evil that lay in the assertion. . .of the immutable and eternal character of their ideas. Because of this latter fact, the laissez faire doctrine was held. . .to express the very order of nature itself. The outcome was the degradation of the idea of individuality until in the minds of many who are themselves struggling for a wider and fuller development of individuality, individualism has become a term of hissing and reproach, while many can see no remedy for the evils that have come from the use of socially unrestrained liberty in business enterprise, save changes produced by violence" ("The Future of Liberalism," *The Later Works of John Dewey*, vol. 11, p. 291).

[29] Dewey, *Ethics, The Later Works*, vol. 7, p. 335.

[30] Dewey, *Ethics, The Later Works*, vol. 7, p. 360. See also *Liberalism and Social Action, The Later Works*, vol. 11, pp. 43-47. Although in somewhat different terms, Dewey, in *Individualism, Old and New*, suggests that the coercive power of capitalism lies in the threat that failure to support existing economic relations will jeopardize social progress. "Speeded-up mass production demands increased buying. It is promoted by advertising on a vast scale, by installment selling, by agents skilled in breaking down sales resistance. Hence buying becomes an economic 'duty' which is as

consonant with the present epoch as thrift was with the period of individualism. For the industrial mechanism depends upon maintaining some kind of an equilibrium between production and consumption. If the equilibrium is disturbed, the whole social structure is affected and prosperity ceases to have a meaning" (*The Later Works*, vol. 5, p. 62).

[31] John Dewey, *Democracy and Education: An Introduction to The Philosophy of Education* (New York: The Macmillan Company, 1916/1950): pp. 16-17.

[32] See Chapter Five, "Habit as Social Practice: A Means for Judging Power," pp. 55-63.

[33] Dewey, *The Study of Ethics: A Syllabus, The Early Works*, vol. 4, p. 248.

[34] Dewey, "Authority and Social Change," *The Later Works*, vol. 11, p. 134.

[35] See Chapter Five, pp. 63-65.

[36] Dewey, "Liberalism and Equality," *The Later Works*, vol. 11, p. 368.

[37] Dewey, *Liberalism and Social Action, The Later Works*, vol. 11, pp. 35-36.

[38] Dewey, "Democracy and Education in the World of Today," *The Later Works*, vol. 13, p. 295.

[39] John Dewey, "Creative Democracy—The Task Before Us," *John Dewey, The Later Works, 1925-1953*, vol. 14, edited by Jo Ann Boydston (Carbondale: Southern Illinois University Press, 1988): p. 228.

[40] Dewey, *Freedom and Culture, The Later Works*, vol. 13, p. 187.

[41] Dewey writes in *Ethics* that "there is a moral tragedy inherent in efforts to further the common good which prevent the result from being either good or common—not good, because it is at the expense of the active growth of those to be helped, and not common because these have no share in bringing the result about. The social welfare can be advanced only by means which enlist the positive interest and active energy of those to be benefited or improved. . . .But without active cooperation both in forming aims and in carrying them out there is no possibility of a common good" (*The Later Works*, vol. 7, p. 347).

[42] Dewey, "Creative Democracy—The Task Before Us," *The Later Works*, vol. 14, p. 227.

[43] Dewey, *Freedom and Culture, The Later Works*, vol. 13, p. 187.

[44] Dewey, *Ethics, The Later Works*, vol. 7, p. 290-291.

[45] Dewey, *Ethics, The Later Works*, vol. 7, p. 230.

[46] Dewey, *Ethics, The Later Works*, vol. 7, pp. 304-305.

[47] Dewey, *Freedom and Culture, The Later Works*, vol. 13, p. 188. In *Ethics* Dewey issues a constant alert: "As soon as one enemy of inquiry and public discussion is overcome, new enemies with new plausible reasons for exercising censorship and suppression of thought arise" (*The Later Works*, vol. 7, p. 231).

[48] Dewey, *Freedom and Culture, The Later Works*, vol. 13, p. 152.

[49] Dewey, "A Liberal Speaks Out for Liberalism," *The Later Works*, vol. 11, pp. 287-288.

[50] Dewey, *Experience and Education*, (1938), *John Dewey, The Later Works, 1925-1953*, vol. 13, edited by Jo Ann Boydston (Carbondale: Southern Illinois University Press, 1988): pp. 31-47, 168-169; "Education and Social Change," *The Later Works*, vol. 11, p. 416.

THE NECESSITY OF EDUCATION TO DEMOCRATIC POWER

As is made clear in Chapter Seven, democracy requires not only courageous involvement but also the honest and open sharing of ideas such that each individual alerts, informs, and enriches the lives of others. To Dewey, the identification of power is a necessary but not a sufficient task in releasing individual capacities to expand and enrich the meaning of the common good. Illuminating the effects of power within shared activity serves as a beginning, not an end, for a public to form a definite idea of itself. Perception of effects on shared habit is an occasion to exchange and judge differing ideas, to fill out and correct competing perspectives. It provides an opportunity for individuals to come to consciousness of those influencing associations of which they are unaware, such that possibilities of growth in interests, desires, capacities, and resources are suggested and shared. As Dewey maintains, "Democracy is itself an educational principle, an educational measure and policy," insofar as education means fostering, cultivating, and sharpening individual capacities through communication.[1] Through the constant give and take of ideas, mere association can tighten into a community in which the activity of each is referred with interest to the activities of others.

In the broadest sense, then, democracy rests upon the working faith that community life is infinitely more powerful in securing a just balance between individual freedom and social equality than is any other mode of associated living. Education serves as the most conscious and surest means by which this faith can be nourished in principle and birthed as a living power through individual character. As Dewey puts it, "Democracy has to be born anew every generation, and education is its midwife."[2]

This chapter will underscore the necessity of a democratic education in light of the understanding that human beings are always in relations of power, the significance of which depends upon human perception and judgment of the actual and potential consequences on the growth of shared habits. Consequently, this chapter will stress the necessity of seeing education as an inherently political undertaking, insofar as education refers to the conscious deliberation about and struggle over valued ends, shared activities, and, thus, forms of power to be fostered or expunged from collective experience. Since education is concerned with the specific forms of community life that should be brought about, an adequate democratic theory of education demands a careful consideration for the consequences of these forms on individual growth, which in turn demands an increased sensitivity for expectations and claims of right intrinsic to these forms. In other words, democratic education inextricably is involved in the struggle over power, over what democratic justice should mean and how this meaning should be cultivated in the characters who will be entrusted with its realization and direction. Therefore, this chapter will emphasize Dewey's point that the ideal of democratic justice can be realized only to the degree that schools aim to cultivate socially and politically engaged citizens who are sympathetically and critically responsive to the demand of democratic justice as it is manifested through the particular activities in which they take part. Furthermore, it will make the pedagogical point that only by engaging individuals to take up the actual social, economic, and political problems that affect them in every phase of their lives can a democratic education develop citizens sensitively, intelligently, and responsibly charged enough to fight hegemonic relations that preclude individual freedom and social equality and to struggle over the meaning of democratic community.

THE PHILISOPHICAL WARRANT FOR A DEMOCRATIC THEORY OF EDUCATION

Every theory of education rests upon philosophical assumptions that provide foundational warrant for its normative prescriptions. The preceding chapters of this study serve as an explicit statement of philosophical warrant for a democratic theory of education. Only a brief summary of the availing points of these chapters is necessary to focus attention on the theory of education that follows.

This study has stressed the fact that human beings ineluctably share in concrete activities that yield concrete results. Simply put, shared activities provide human beings with the fundamental means of living and learning. They are the essential substances through which individuals acquire and refine their special affections, dexterities, and aptitudes. They are the media by which individuals more or less develop a sense of the shared goods directing their effective capacities and of the common standards, expectations, and claims of right by which to judge their efforts and sharpen their judgments. Fundamentally, shared habit is social power, the ability to act so as to affect the social environment, the growth and direction of which depends directly upon the human responsibility to define and measure the moral significance of its execution. That is, the determination of power (effective capacity) as enhancing or debilitating rests upon some character attempting to discover and judge the consequences of a particular line of conduct on the growth of his interests, skills, desires, habits, and ways of forming ends and on the shared arrangements, opportunities, and materials that nourish the active participation and growth of others.

Variation of social environment and practices, however, cultivates a variety of interests, valued ends, and habits of attention and judgment. Experience is shot through with competing judgments over the relative value of power. As Dewey suggests, social conflict is a fundamental datum. In light of all evidence that the growth and direction of human experience is not determined by any metaphysical absolutes or necessities, ill will and selfishness are just as ontologically possible as goodwill and altruism. Stated differently, human beings are just as capable of manipulating each other's needs, desires, wants, and ways of judgment to serve and legitimize narrow, selfish ends as they are capable of directing each other to search and act for ends that appreciate in value and expand the lives of all. According to

Dewey's philosophical account of human conduct, individuals always <u>should</u> act so as to stimulate the growth of their own capacities with due care for the particular claims, needs, well-being, and development of others. This is to suggest that the moral significance of any form of power <u>should</u> be judged according to the extent to which it expands and enriches the meaning of individual liberty in just relation to the meaning of social equality.

It also has been suggested that the quest for an enriched democratic justice requires free flowing and broad communication about the consequences of shared activity. Mutual reference and exchange of ideas is vital for multiplying perceptions of possible resources, sharpening consciousness of shared ends, and stoking the desire to excel beyond existing conceptions of good. Constant vigilance over existing efforts to meet social demands helps detect conditions that set up unequal relations of power and that stifle freedom of individual growth in effect. Persistent questioning and shared, critical inquiry help bring debilitating forms of power that coerce acceptance of supporting conditions to the light of social discussion and deliberation. However, the work of democracy does not take place merely by virtue of collective acceptance and general appeal to its abstract principles. The work of democracy can be made concrete, secured, refined, and extended only through the day in and day out activities that human beings share. As Dewey suggests, "Only when we start from a community as a fact, grasp the fact in thought so as to clarify and enhance its constituent elements, can we reach an idea of democracy which is not utopian. The conceptions and shibboleths which are traditionally associated with the idea of democracy take on veridical and directive meaning only when they are construed as marks and traits of an association which realizes the defining characteristics of a community."[3]

Democracy as a moral ideal, therefore, challenges each individual to be actively engaged with the particular problems that arise within his various associations and that limit free and full contact with each other. Only through active concern for the community of good in which one is a part can problems be immediately felt, understood, and appreciated with sympathy. Only through constant communication and critical reflection about shared ends and purposes, standards, and the special needs and capacities of all involved can existing efforts to satisfy social needs be measured, deficiencies be identified, and further work be suggested. Only when felt problems are communicated can a public form to discuss the value of existing power and, therefore, suggest and debate what forms of power are worth promoting or resisting. To deliberate about the forms of power to promote is to struggle over what effective capacities should be cultivated. As Dewey suggests, to struggle over effective capacities is to struggle over what liberty should mean in the concrete and, by implication, what equality and justice should mean as well.

> Liberty is not just an idea, an abstract principle. It is power, effective power to do specific things. There is no such thing as liberty in general; liberty, so to speak, at large. If one wants to know what the condition of liberty is at a given time, one has to examine what persons can do and what they cannot do. The moment one examines the question from the standpoint of effective

action, it becomes evident that the demand for liberty is a demand for power, either for possession of powers of action not already possessed or for retention and expansion of powers already possessed. . . .Demand for increased power at one point means demands for change in the distribution of powers, that is, for less power somewhere else. You cannot discuss or measure the liberty of one individual or group of individuals without thereby raising the question of the effect upon the liberty of others. . . .Liberty is always a social question, not an individual one. For the liberties that any individual actually has depends upon the distribution of powers or liberties that exits, and this distribution is identical with actual social arrangements, legal and political –and, at the present time, economic, in a peculiarly important way.[4]

In the most basic sense, then, to be actively concerned for and engaged in the struggle for liberty is to take part in the discussion about what kind of community should be in the making and what sort of citizens are necessary to see it to fruition. This is to reiterate, with Dewey, that democracy demands nothing more or less than social and political engagement in the direction of shared experience. Thus, an education most fitting to democracy is one that consciously aims to cultivate "robust trustees of its own resources and ideals."[5] That is, a democratic education must develop citizens with the affections, skills, intelligence, and virtues (effective habits or powers) necessary to assume social and political responsibility for seeking freedom in just relation with equality. Therefore, democratic education implies a political education.

A DEMOCRATIC THEORY OF EDUCATION

As Dewey points out, "The problem of education in its relation to direction of social change is all one with the problem of finding out what democracy means in its total range of concrete applications: economic, domestic, international, religious, cultural, and political."[6] Insofar as democracy entails finding out what freedom and equality mean in a just relation with each other, then the ongoing problem of democratic justice—the problem of equalizing power—gives a general direction to the aims and methods of democratic education. The problem of justice demands that schools cultivate character animated by social interests and sympathy and guided by social intelligence.

A character animated by social interests and sympathy refers to an individual who consciously appreciates the inherent social nature of human existence. To appreciate is to feel and understand the quality of something, to sense its goods and standards. To appreciate the inherent social nature of existence entails the further recognition that human beings are creatures of acquired habit, the good of which should be a more refined and controlled interaction with the social environment. More specifically, it entails the conscious sense that human beings are living organisms whose life-sustaining activities are directly dependent upon the activities of others for formation, sustenance, and growth. To appreciate the social nature of humankind is to understand the fact that the growth of an individual can be secured only as he or she takes in, digests, and replenishes the social nutrients that sustain him or her. This is to recognize that the good of growth can be realized only as the individual attends to the particular aims, purposes, and skills of others, as well as to their demands to realize the good in a way that is considerate and careful of their particular needs and development. In the most fundamental sense, to appreciate the inherent social nature of human existence is to understand the basic fact that individual liberty or freedom to grow always involves the matter of a just relation with others who make up the social environment and who share in the consequences of growth. It is to recognize that the meaning of the good always should be a social good, the expansion of which depends upon increasing the range and depth of sympathy one has for the needs, expectations, and demands of others. As Dewey suggests, "To put ourselves in the place of another, to see things from the standpoint of his aims and values, to humble our estimate of our own pretensions to the level they assume in the eyes of an impartial observer, is the surest way to appreciate what justice demands in concrete cases."[7] A character motivated by social interests, furthermore, is one charged by an affection for social well being and by a "hatred for all that hinders this well-being."[8] Like all interests, a social interest signifies something active, in this case, an active search for the concrete opportunities that expand and enrich mutual contact, as well as an active search for the arrangements that preclude, shut down, and distort free and open communication. By implication, then, a social interest suggests a special sensitivity for the persistent problems that plague shared activities and a special affection for the "underdog" who suffers most in consequence of these problems. In the most general sense, a character animated by social interests has not only an acute feel for the concrete problem of justice but a strong sense of responsibility for the conduct that causes and changes this problem. A sense of social welfare, as Dewey implies, induces a sense of responsibility, a sense of the necessity to know and reflect upon the conditions and consequences of conduct. "The tendency, moreover, of adopting social well-being as a standard is to make us intellectually sensitive and critical about the effects of laws, social arrangements, and education upon human happiness and development."[9]

Simply put, intelligence refers to the effective power or capacity to search and obtain adequate knowledge of actual and potential conditions so as to conduct oneself more effectively and efficiently. Dewey suggests that intelligence refers to the "active, persistent, and careful consideration of any belief or supposed form of knowledge in the light of the grounds that support it and the further conclusions to which it tends."[10] More specifically, intelligence denotes a certain habit of mental attention that brings the how and why of conduct into immediate focus through the light of past experience. It is the inquiry into and identification of the "consequence" of ideas and facts for the purpose of judging the degree to which each grows out of and supports the occurrence of the others. Social intelligence, then, refers to the power of forming and judging the means and consequences of conduct on the growth of shared habits and conditions. Fundamentally, social intelligence signifies the social control of conduct mediated through individual character.

A character guided by social intelligence strives to be more perceptive, reflective, and judicious about the effects of conduct on the equal consideration and just development of all involved. This is to say, the problem of justice (again, the problem of equalizing power) fixes not only the end of social intelligence but its means as well. To approach the problem of justice by way of social intelligence requires certain attitudes or traits of character and modes of approach. Gaining adequate knowledge requires a skeptical attitude towards the surface or apparent meaning of facts. It requires an insistent desire for a range of facts and evidence and an openness of mind to consider fully the significance of facts as reported from as many different perspectives as possible. Thus, social intelligence entails a willingness to endure suspense and uncertainty of outcome until enough facts have been identified and mined for their concrete bearings. To act with social intelligence demands a tolerance or willingness to attend to and face the reported meanings of facts with sincerity, no matter how congruent or conflicting these are with some particular interest. Furthermore, since the problem of democratic justice demands the consideration of facts according to the needs and claims of others, then justice requires a character willing to seek out the perspectives of others as indispensable resources for guidance.

As a mode of address, social intelligence refers to the reliance upon mutual communication and reference, the free and open exchange of ideas, as the most equitable and accurate way to detect and deliberate about the concrete problems of enriching the liberties of all. It is the practice of building up and consulting with a tribunal of others as diverse and rich in experience as possible. Social intelligence denotes the method of meeting with others in order to inquire into, correct, and round out ideas and suggestions. It is the means by which to sharpen judgments about the relative values of facts, active habits, and the distribution of power. This is to say, social intelligence refers to the way of collectively acquiring and directing a stronger sense of social well being—intelligent sympathy.

As Dewey suggests, only by aiming to cultivate characters guided by intelligence and sympathy can a democratic society thrive. "Only as the coming generation learns in the schools to understand the social forces that are at work, the directions and the cross-directions in which they are moving, the consequences that they are reproducing, the consequences that they might produce if they were understood and managed with intelligence –only as the schools provide this understanding, have we any assurance that they are meeting the challenge which is put to them by democracy."[11] The pedagogical implication that follows is that critical, democratic habits of mind can form and mature only as they are fed constantly through practice. Thus, the only way to cultivate characters who will be actively engaged in the challenge of democracy is to engage them in the concrete challenges of justice. Therefore, a democratic education requires several important responsibilities of the schools in terms of the conditions, methods, and content of instruction.

SCHOOL CONTEXT

First, the school must provide a context that ensures intellectual freedom and encourages shared inquiry, communication and deliberation. All those concerned with public education must be involved and vigilant in detecting relations of power that, intentionally or not, prevent, censor, or distort the freedom of inquiry, discussion, and expression. However, the identification of merely restrictive forms of power is not enough. Dewey's reminder that powerful groups have influenced shared institutions so as to condition others to accept, desire, and blindly act for ends antithetical to the growth of personal freedom should give a more critical edge to the watchdog responsibilities of the public. The possibility that powerful ill-willed individuals can –and, in fact, do—use the public schools to gain hegemonic control over perspective should make all concerned about a public education more wary and discriminating of the vested interests that permeate schools. Of course, the relative effect and value of power are matters of judgment and, therefore, matters to be contested and debated. This is to say that education necessarily is involved in the larger political discussion about what kind of community should be in the making. It is immersed in the collective deliberation and struggle over the effects of existing power on the growth of freedom; the types of associations or powers that should be fostered; and the habits of character necessary to develop these associations into conscious communities of good. A primary responsibility of all those committed to a democratic education (especially administrators, teachers, and parents) is to make sure that the school serves as the best example of democracy in the political engagement about the direction of experience. This responsibility entails making the school a citadel for the methods indispensable to a thriving cultural and political democracy. If schools are to produce active political citizens, the atmosphere of the school must be saturated with a spirit of public participation and civic courage. "It is idle to expect the schools to send out young men and women who will stand actively and aggressively for the cause of free intelligence in meeting social problems and attaining the goal of freedom unless the spirit of free intelligence pervades the organization, administration, studies, and methods of the school itself. . . .Eternal vigilance is the price of the conservation and extension of freedom, and the schools should be the ceaseless guardians and creators of this vigilance."[12]

CONTEXT AND METHODS OF INSTRUCTION

As Dewey points out above, securing a context that is conducive to intellectual freedom is one element in the shaping of characters who are able to form ideas that are socially relevant. Therefore, the second responsibility of the schools is to provide an organized set of experiences that socially and politically engages students such that critical, intelligent sympathy develops as a necessary habit of practice. Dewey's 1922 criticism of public schools in terms of their instructional duties is worth quoting at length because it offers a timeless suggestion for what the general content and methods of democratic schools should be.

Our schooling does not educate, if by education be meant a trained habit of discriminating inquiry and discriminating belief, the ability to look beneath a floating surface to detect the conditions that fix the contour of the surface, and the forces which create its waves and drifts. . . .This fact determines the fundamental criticism to be leveled against current schooling, against what passes as an educational system.   It not only does little to make discriminating intelligence a safeguard against surrender to the invasion of bunk, especially in its most dangerous form –social and political bunk—but it does much to favor susceptibility to a welcoming reception of it.   There appear to be two chief causes for this ineptitude.   One is the persistence, in the body of what is taught, of traditional material which. . .affords no resource for discriminating insight, no protection against being duped in facing the emergencies of today. . . .The other way in which schooling fosters an undiscriminating gulping mental habit, eager to be duped, is positive.   It consists in a systematic, almost deliberate, avoidance of the spirit of criticism in dealing with history, politics, and economics.   There is an implicit belief that this avoidance is the only way by which to produce good citizens.   The more undiscriminating the history and institutions of one's own nation are idealized, the greater is the likelihood, so it is assumed, that the school product will be a loyal patriot, a well-equipped good citizen.   If the average boy and girl could be walled off from all ideas and information about social affairs save those acquired in school, they would enter upon the responsibilities of social membership in complete ignorance that there are any social problems, any political evils, any industrial defects. They would go forth with the supreme confidence that the way lies open to all, and that the sole cause of failure in business, family life or citizenship lies in some personal deficiency in character. . . .The effect is to send students out into actual life in a condition of acquired and artificial innocence.   Such perceptions as they may have of the realities of social struggles and problems they have derived incidentally, by the way, and without the safeguards of intelligent acquaintance with facts and impartially conducted discussion.   It is no wonder that they are ripe to be gulled, or that their attitude is one which merely perpetuates existing confusion, ignorance, prejudice, and credulity.   Reaction from this impossible naïve idealization of institutions as they are produces indifference and cynicism.[13]

To produce good citizens, that is, individuals who are sympathetic and responsible for the direction of experience, requires supplying the concrete opportunities that will call these traits out as genuine, active responses. It follows that the subject-matter of education can be nothing less than shared experience itself.   Since shared experience fundamentally consists of share habits and practices, then in the most elemental sense, the curricular and instructional responsibilities of the school must be to widen and enrich the students' native interest in the social activities that compose their particular community of experience. This should be done by enlisting all students' energies in trying out and undergoing a myriad of practices that will enhance their natural sensitivity to and curiosity for what their community life is like.

The importance of shared practices for curriculum and instruction cannot be overstated. As pointed out throughout this study, shared practices develop in response to the particular problems and demands of the social environment. Thus, they are the particular means to realize specific consequences in experience. Again, as Dewey plainly states it, "Concrete habits do all the perceiving, recognizing, imagining, recalling, judging, conceiving, and reasoning that is done."[14] They are the special powers by which to form and regulate experience with efficiency and meaning. Furthermore, shared practices are the forms of human association. They serve as the mechanisms by which to realize further connections with other forms of human activity and to understand the intimate interactions between people that make community life possible and important. Directly engaging students in the concrete activities of community life provides the best stimulus to induce students to find out what the special demands and purposes of community life are. In turn, a developing sense of shared ends and demands gives social purpose to the need to acquire special methods for gathering facts and generating ideas and for developing special techniques and skills necessary to execute plans. A sense of shared ideals and demands gives reason for the need to attend to and judge consequences more carefully and to modify plans in light of their consequences. As Dewey suggests, "Things gain meaning when they are used as means to bring about consequences (or as means to prevent the occurrence of undesired consequences), or as standing for consequences for which we have to discover means. The relation of means-consequence is the centre and heart of all understanding."[15] On the most elementary level, therefore, the school should involve students in shared activities such that the means-consequence relation and the inherent human responsibility for this relation becomes the constant integrating theme of their educational experience. The different content areas of the traditional curriculum represent the various ways of approaching this relation and therefore represent the different ways of stating, analyzing, and understanding it. It follows that all subsequent efforts in terms of instructional content and method should bring the social significance of the means-consequence relation to greater degrees of consciousness. This is to say, the elementary development of attention through shared practices has instructional significance for engaging students to take up the problem of democratic justice.

As pointed out above, shared practices are the particular means to specific consequences in the social environment. When transferred into personal ability, shared practices are effective capacities, liberties, or, to put it in more relevant terms, powers to act. Since liberties always produce social effects, liberties always entail the social question of justice, the question of harmonious balance between the capacities of one and the capacities of all. Directly engaging students in the means-consequence relation that makes up the central nerve of shared practices furnishes the most direct mechanism by which students can develop an intimate sensitivity to and personal responsibility for the problem of justice in its various concrete manifestations.

The problem for instruction is selecting and arranging the experiences necessary to lead students to define the good of a particular activity and to develop a sense of what expectations and demands should guide their consideration of consequences and means. By way of developing an idea of goods and standards, students come to sense for themselves the special problems and conflicts intrinsic to a particular shared activity. That is, a developing interest in realizing a particular shared good provides the prime condition for a heightened sensitivity and attention to the ideas, beliefs, and relations that block or hinder the full satisfaction of the good. As students are engaged in forming and measuring shared goods, they implicitly are forming and judging powers and consequences, liberty and equality –justice. The role of the teacher becomes that of suggesting and magnifying the social, economic, and political implications of felt problems such that questions of justice serve explicitly as stimuli to call out and sharpen social intelligence as a response.

In the most basic sense, the role of the teacher is to serve as a resource for suggestion and guidance. The instructional task, then, includes directing students in bringing felt problems to a more acute, articulated focus by suggesting and supplying additional materials, accounts, and claims to be researched. This function entails leading students into a careful study of the history of particular problems to see what specific events and assumptions of meaning inform their manifestations. Thus, the teacher should serve as a model for sound habits of investigation. This involves helping students search for and gather relevant facts, and examine and test the relations between facts so as to induce a clearer understanding of the particular ideas of good and demands of right these facts embody or ignore. But, more specifically in terms of power, the teacher carries the responsibility of making explicit the point that underlying ideas of good and right represent specific relations of power, specific ideas of liberty or effective capacity, specific demands for increased capacity, constrained capacity, or redistributed capacity. The job of the teacher is to help students uncover and untangle the particular interests served by relations of power as these are embedded in historical facts and have come to bear upon presently felt problems. Therefore, the more critical and political aspect of teaching is directing students in identifying, deliberating about, and judging the effects of power on the development of shared habits, desires, needs, and ways of judgment. This task involves leading students in tracing out and examining the particular means used to legitimize one way of acting, one form of power, over another. Of course, engaging students in these political tasks depends upon the creative ability to select experiences that will lead students to identify problems extensive enough in social scope so as to require them to seek out the perspectives of others, both historical and current. Therefore, another responsibility of teaching is to help students build a wider and more enriched forum of community experience.

By use of the extensive nature of the problem of justice itself, the teacher must lead students to see that only as they draw upon the lived experiences and stories of others can they gather a range of facts and judgments necessary to bring particular injustices into adequate focus. Therefore, it is incumbent upon the teacher to cultivate in students a strong sense that only as they seek out the perspectives of others can they come to hear and feel a variety of living testaments of past events, episodes, and effects of power. Mutual reference, in turn, should lend an emotional charge and significance to students' intellectual search, particularly as they struggle to identify and measure competing ideas of good and right. What students should come to see is that free and open discussion serves as a vital means by which they may become alert to subtle forms of exploitation that they had not yet taken into account. An intimate exchange of perspective should serve as the indispensable medium by which students come to confront the consequences of exploitation as these are manifested in impulses, desires, and ways of judgment. Through mutual conference students can come to help each other demystify hegemonic forms of power as natural and outside of human change. Moreover, drawing upon the stories of others should allow students to come to consciousness of past struggles of protest and resistance. In turn, these past struggles should provide rich suggestions as to how to form effective coalitions of resistance against current injustices and offer insights about how to nourish more intimate associations with others. Therefore, the teacher's duty in this regard is to underscore the significance of assembling a tribunal of others that will act as an authoritative resource by which students can come to test, correct, and sharpen their ideas of the good to be served and the responsibilities inherent in serving it.

The upshot of this discussion leads to a simple but indispensable educational principle. As Dewey states it, "The only way to prepare for social life is to engage in social life. To form habits of social usefulness and serviceableness apart from any direct social need and motive, and apart from any existing social situation, is, to the letter, teaching the child to swim by going through motions outside of the water. The most indispensable condition is left out, and the results correspondingly futile."[16] Thus, the only sure way to foster democratic characters able to identify hegemonic forms of power and to struggle to improve social conditions is to engage individuals in active struggles for social, economic, and political justice that will give their incipient habits real outlet. This is to say that the work of democracy cannot be undertaken, not to mention realized, simply by telling students what democracy has meant in the past and should mean in the future. In order for it to survive, democracy cannot be simply just another civics lesson; it has to be an active way of life. According to Dewey, "Every generation has to accomplish democracy over again for itself; that its very nature, its essence, is something that cannot be handed on from one person or generation to another, but has to be worked out in terms of needs, problems, and conditions of the social life of which, as the years go by, we are a part."[17]

NOTES

[1] John Dewey, "Democracy and Education in the World of Today," *John Dewey, The Later Works, 1925-1953*, vol. 13, edited by Jo Ann Boydston (Carbondale: Southern Illinois University Press, 1988): p. 294.

[2] John Dewey, "The Need of an Industrial Education in an Industrial Democracy," *John Dewey, The Middle Works, 1899-1924*, vol. 10, edited by Jo Ann Boydston (Carbondale: Southern Illinois University Press, 1980): p. 139.

[3] John Dewey, *The Public and Its Problems* (Chicago: The Swallow Press, 1927/1954): p. 149.

[4] John Dewey, "Liberty and Social Control," *John Dewey, The Later Works, 1925-1953*, vol. 11, edited by Jo Ann Boydston (Carbondale: Southern Illinois University Press, 1987): pp. 360-362. In "The Social Significance of Academic Freedom," Dewey writes, "Liberty is a social matter and not just a claim of the private individual. Freedom is a matter of the distribution of effective power; the struggle for liberty is important because of its consequences in effecting more just, equable, and human relations of men, women, and children to one another" (*The Later Works*, vol. 11, p. 377).

[5] John Dewey, *Democracy and Education: An Introduction to The Philosophy of Education* (New York: The Macmillan Company, 1916/1950): p. 12.

[6] John Dewey, "Education and Social Change," *The Later Works*, vol. 11, p. 416.

[7] John Dewey and James Hayden Tufts, *Ethics* (1908/1932), *John Dewey, The Later Works, 1925-1953*, vol. 7, edited by Jo Ann Boydston (Carbondale: Southern Illinois University Press, 1985): p. 251.

[8] John Dewey, *Psychology* (1887), *John Dewey, The Early Works, 1882-1898*, vol. 2, edited by Jo Ann Boydston (Carbondale: Southern Illinois University Press, 1967): p. 293.

[9] John Dewey, *Ethics, The Later Works*, vol. 7, p. 251.

[10] John Dewey, *How We Think: A Restatement of the Relation of Reflective Thinking to the Educative Process* (1910/1933), *John Dewey, The Later Works, 1925-1953*, vol. 8, edited by Jo Ann Boydston (Carbondale: Southern Illinois University Press, 1986): p. 118. See also pp. 113-124.

[11] John Dewey, "The Challenge of Democracy to Education," *The Later Works*, vol. 11, p. 183.

[12] John Dewey, "Freedom," *The Later Works*, vol. 11, pp. 254-255.

[13] John Dewey, "Education as Politics," *John Dewey, The Middle Works, 1899-1924*, vol. 13, edited by Jo Ann Boydston (Carbondale: Southern Illinois University Press, 1983): pp. 331-333.

[14] John Dewey, *Human Nature and Conduct: An Introduction to Social Psychology* (New York: The Modern Library, 1922/1930): p. 177.

[15] John Dewey, *How We Think, The Later Works*, vol. 8, p. 233.

[16] John Dewey, "Ethical Principles Underlying Education," *John Dewey, The Early Works, 1882-1898*, vol. 5, edited by Jo Ann Boydston (Carbondale: Southern Illinois University Press, 1972): p. 62.

[17] John Dewey, "Democracy and Education in the World of Today," *The Later Works*, vol. 13, p. 299.

Previously published as:

Democratic Education: A Deweyan Inspired Reminder by Randall Hewitt E&C/Education and Culture, The Journal of the John Dewey Society for the Study of Education and Culture, Volume 22, Issue 2 © *2006 Purdue University Press*

REFERENCES

Anderson, Quentin. (1992). John Dewey's American Democrat. In *John Dewey: Critical Assessments II*, edited by J. E. Tiles. New York: Routledge, 91-108.

Apple, Michael. (1990). *Ideology and Curriculum*, second edition. New York: Routledge.

Barber, Benjamin. (1995/2001). *Jihad Vs. McWorld: Terrorism's Challenge to Democracy*. NewYork: Ballantine Books.

Bernstein, Richard. (1991). *The New Constellation: The Ethical-Political Horizons of Modernity/ Postmodernity*. Cambridge, Massachusetts: The MIT Press.

_____. (1976). *The Restructuring of Social and Political Theory*. Philadelphia, Pennsylvania: University of Pennsylvania Press.

_____. (1986). *Philosophical Profiles: Essays in a Pragmatic Mode*. Philadelphia, Pennsylvania: University of Pennsylvania Press.

Bowles, Samuel and Herbert Gintis. (1976). *Schooling in Capital America: Educational Reform and the Contradictions of Economic Life*. New York: Basic Books.

Campbell, James. (1995). *Understanding John Dewey: Nature and Cooperative Intelligence*. Chicago: Open Court Publishing Company.

Counts, George S. (1932). *Dare the School Build a New Social Order?* New York: John Day.

Crosser, Paul. (1955). *The Nihilism of John Dewey*. New York: Philosophical Library, Inc.

Dewey, John. (1987). Authority and Social Change. *John Dewey: The Later Works, 1925-1953*, vol. 11, edited by Jo Ann Boydston. Carbondale, Illinois: Southern Illinois University Press, 130-145.

_____. (1987). The Challenge of Democracy to Education. *John Dewey: The Later Works, 1925-1953*, vol. 11, edited by Jo Ann Boydston. Carbondale, Illinois: Southern Illinois University Press, 181-190.

Dewey, John. (1988). Creative Democracy—The Task Before Us. *John Dewey: The Later Works, 1925-1953*, vol. 14, edited by Jo Ann Boydston. Carbondale, Illinois: Southern Illinois University Press, 224-230.

_____. (1916/1950). *Democracy and Education: An Introduction to The Philosophy of Education*. New York: The Macmillan Company.

_____. (1988). Democracy and Education in the World of Today. *John Dewey: TheLater Works, 1925-1953*, vol. 13, edited by Jo Ann Boydston. Carbondale, Illinois: Southern Illinois University Press, 294-303.

_____. (1987). Education and Social Change. *John Dewey: The Later Works, 1925-1953*, vol. 11, edited by Jo Ann Boydston. Carbondale, Illinois: Southern Illinois University Press, 408-417.

_____. (1983). Education as Politics. *John Dewey: The Middle Works, 1899- 1924* vol. 13, edited by Jo Ann Boydston. Carbondale, Illinois: Southern Illinois University Press, 329-334.

_____. (1972). Ethical Principles Underlying Education. *John Dewey: The Early Works, 1882-1898*, vol. 5, edited by Jo Ann Boydston. Carbondale, Illinois: Southern Illinois University Press, 54-83.

_____. (1938/1988). *Experience and Education. John Dewey: The Later Works, 1925-1953*, vol. 13, edited by Jo Ann Boydston. Carbondale, Illinois: Southern Illinois University Press, 1-62.

_____. (1925/1958). *Experience and Nature*. New York: Dover Publications, Inc.

_____. (1980). Force, Violence, and Law. *John Dewey: The Middle Works, 1899-1924*, vol. 10, edited by Jo Ann Boydston. Carbondale, Illinois: Southern Illinois University Press, 211-215.

_____. (1987). Freedom. *John Dewey: The Later Works, 1925-1953*, vol. 11, edited by Jo Ann Boydston. Carbondale, Illinois: Southern Illinois University Press, 247-255.

_____. (1939/1988). *Freedom and Culture. John Dewey: The Later Works, 1925-1953*, vol. 13, edited by Jo Ann Boydston. Carbondale, Illinois: Southern Illinois University Press, 63-188.

REFERENCES

Dewey, John (1984). From Absolutism to Experimentalism. *John Dewey: The Later Works, 1925-1953*, vol. 5, edited by Jo Ann Boydston. Carbondale, Illinois: Southern Illinois University Press, 147-160.

_____. (1987). The Future of Liberalism. *John Dewey: The Later Works, 1925- 1953*, vol. 11, edited by Jo Ann Boydston. Carbondale, Illinois: Southern Illinois University Press, 289-295.

_____. (1922/1930). *Human Nature and Conduct: An Introduction to Social Psychology*. New York: Random House.

_____. (1910/1933/1986). *How We Think: A Restatement of the Relation of Reflective Thinking to the Educative Process. John Dewey: The Later Works, 1925-1953*, vol. 8, edited by Jo Ann Boydston. Carbondale, Illinois: Southern Illinois University Press, 105-352.

_____. (1929/1984). *Individualism, Old and New. John Dewey: The Later Works, 1925-1953*, vol. 5, edited by Jo Ann Boydston. Carbondale, Illinois: Southern Illinois University Press, 41-123.

_____. (1979). *Interest and Effort in Education. John Dewey: The MiddleWorks, 1899-1924*, vol. 7, edited by Jo Ann Boydston. Carbondale, Illinois: Southern Illinois University Press, 151-197.

_____. (1969). Kant and Philosophic Method. *John Dewey: The Early Works, 1882-1898*, vol. 1, edited by Jo Ann Boydston. Carbondale, Illinois: Southern Illinois University Press, 34-47.

_____. (1969). Knowledge and The Relativity of Feeling. *John Dewey: The Early Works, 1882-1898*, vol. 1, edited by Jo Ann Boydston. Carbondale, Illinois: Southern Illinois University Press, 19-33.

_____. (1987). A Liberal Speaks Out for Liberalism. *John Dewey: The Later   Works, 1925-1953*, vol. 11, edited by Jo Ann Boydston. Carbondale, Illinois: Southern Illinois University Press, 282-288.

_____. (1987). Liberalism and Equality. *John Dewey: The Later Works, 1925- 1953*, vol. 11, edited by Jo Ann Boydston. Carbondale, Illinois: Southern Illinois University Press, 368-371.

_____. (1935/1987). *Liberalism and Social Action. John Dewey: The Later   Works, 1925-1953*, vol. 11, edited by Jo Ann Boydston. Carbondale, Illinois: Southern   Illinois University Press, 1-65.

Dewey, John. (1987). Liberty and Social Control. *John Dewey: The Later Works,   1925-1953*, vol. 11, edited by Jo Ann Boydston. Carbondale, Illinois: Southern   Illinois University Press, 360-363.

_____. (1969). The Metaphysical Assumptions of Materialism. *John Dewey: The Early Works, 1882-1898*, vol. 1, edited by Jo Ann Boydston. Carbondale, Illinois: Southern Illinois University Press, 3-8.

_____.   (1980). The Need of an Industrial Education in an Industrial Democracy. *John Dewey: The Middle Works, 1899-1924*, vol. 10, edited by Jo Ann Boydston. Carbondale, Illinois: Southern Illinois University Press, 137-143.

_____. (1969). The Psychological Standpoint. *John Dewey: The Early Works, 1882-1898*, vol. 1, edited by Jo Ann Boydston. Carbondale, Illinois: Southern Illinois University Press, 122-143.

_____. (1887/1967). *Psychology. John Dewey: The Early Works, 1882-1898*, vol. 2, edited by Jo Ann Boydston. Carbondale, Illinois: Southern Illinois   University Press.

_____. (1969). Psychology as Philosophic Method. *John Dewey: The Early Works, 1882-1898*, vol. 1, edited by Jo Ann Boydston. Carbondale, Illinois: Southern Illinois University Press, 144-167.

_____. (1927/1954*). The Public and Its Problems*. Chicago: The Swallow Press, Inc.

_____. (1920/1949). *Reconstruction In Philosophy*. Boston: The Beacon Press.

_____. (1972). The Reflex Arc Concept in Psychology. *John Dewey: The Early Works, 1882-1898*, vol. 5, edited by Jo Ann Boydston. Carbondale, Illinois: Southern Illinois University Press, 96-109.

_____. (1969). Soul and Body. *John Dewey: The Early Works, 1882-1898*, vol. 1, edited by Jo Ann Boydston. Carbondale, Illinois: Southern Illinois University Press, 93-115.

_____. (1894/1971). *The Study of Ethics: A Syllabus. John Dewey: The Early Works, 1882-1898*, vol. 4, edited by Jo Ann Boydston. Carbondale, Illinois: Southern Illinois University Press, 219-362.

Dewey, John and James Hayden Tufts. (1908/1932/1985). *Ethics, John Dewey: The Later Works, 1925-1953*, vol. 7, edited by Jo Ann Boydston. Carbondale, Illinois: Southern Illinois University Press.

Diggins, John Patrick. (1994). *The Promise of Pragmatism: Modernism and The Crisis of Knowledge and Authority*. Chicago: The University of Chicago Press.

Dykhuizen, George. (1973). *The Life and Mind of John Dewey*, edited by Jo Ann Boydston. Carbondale, Illinois: Southern Illinois University Press.

Eldridge, Michael. (1998). *Transforming Experience: John Dewey's Cultural Instrumentalism*. Nashville, Tennessee: Vanderbilt University Press.

Estremera, Miguel Angel. (1993). *Democratic Theories of Hope: A Critical Comparative Analysis of The Public Philosophies of John Dewey and Henry A. Giroux*, Ph. D. dissertation. New Brunswick: Rutgers The State University of New Jersey.

Flay, Joseph. (1992). Alienation and The Status Quo. *John Dewey: Critical Assessments II*, edited by J. E. Tiles. New York: Routledge, 307-319.

Foucault, Michel. (1972). *The Archaeology of Knowledge and The Discourse on Language*, translated by A. M. Sheridan Smith. New York: Pantheon Books.

_____. (1975). *The Birth of The Clinic: An Archaeology of Medical Perception*, translated by A. M. Sheridan Smith. New York: Vintage Books.

_____. (1979). *Discipline and Punish: The Birth of The Prison*, translated by Alan Sheridan. New York: Vintage Books.

_____. (1980). *Power/Knowledge: Selected Interviews and Other Writings, 1972-1977*, translated and edited by Colin Gordon. New York: Pantheon Books.

Gabriel, Ralph Henry. (1956). *The Course of American Democratic Thought*, Second edition. New York: The Ronald Press Company.

Giroux, Henry. (1988). *Schooling and The Struggle for Public Life: Critical Pedagogy in the Modern Age*. Minneapolis, Minnesota: University of Minnesota Press.

Gouinlock, James. (1972). *John Dewey's Philosophy of Value*. New York: Humanities Press. Greene, Maxine. (1988). *The Dialectic of Freedom*. New York: Teachers College Press.

Gutmann, Amy. (1987). *Democratic Education*. Princeton, New Jersey: Princeton University Press.

Hamilton, William. (1803). Editor's Supplementary Dissertations. *The Philosophical Works of Thomas Reid*, eighth edition, 2 volumes, edited and supplemented by Sir William Hamilton. Edinburgh, Scottland: James Thin.

Harvey, David. (1992). *The Condition of Postmodernity: An Enquiry into the Origins of Cultural Change*. Cambridge, Massachusetts: Blackwell Publishers.

Hegel, Georg Wilhelm Friedrich. (1959). *Encyclopedia of Philosophy*, translated and annotated by Gustav Emil Mueller. New York: Philosophical Library, Inc.

Held, David. (1980). *Introduction to Critical Theory: Horkheimer to Habermas*. Berkeley, California: University of California Press.

James, William. (1909/1975). *The Meaning of Truth: A Sequel to Pragmatism*. Cambridge, Massachusetts: Harvard University Press.

_____. (1907/1975). *Pragmatism: A New Name for Some Old Ways of Thinking*. Cambridge, Massachusetts: Harvard University Press.

_____. (1901-02/1958). *The Varieties of Religious Experience*. New York: Penguin Books.

_____. (1897/1956). *The Will to Believe: And Other Essays in Popular Philosophy*. New York: Dover Publications, Inc.

Kant, Immanuel. (1957). *Kant Selections*, edited by Theodore M. Greene. New York: Charles Scribner's Sons.

Kellner, Douglas. (1989). *Critical Theory, Marxism and Modernity*. Baltimore, Maryland: The Johns Hopkins University Press.

Kirk, Russell. (1953). *The Conservative Mind: From Burke to Santayana*. Chicago: H. Regnery Co.

REFERENCES

Kuklick, Bruce. (1985). *Churchmen and Philosophers: From Jonathan Edwards to John Dewey.* New Haven, Connecticut: Yale University Press.
Kuklick, Bruce. (1977). *The Rise of American Philosophy.* New Haven, Connecticut: Yale University Press.
Laclau, Ernesto and Chantal Mouffe. (1993). *Hegemony and Socialist Strategy: Towards a Radical Democratic Politics.* London and New York: Verso.
Lovejoy, Arthur O. (1963). *The Thirteen Pragmatisms and Other Essays.* Baltimore, Maryland: The Johns Hopkins Press.
Marcuse, Herbert. (1992). John Dewey's *Theory of Valuation.* *John Dewey: Critical Assessments III,* edited by J. E. Tiles. New York: Routledge, 22-27.
McCarthy, Thomas. (1993). *Ideals and Illusions: On Reconstruction and Deconstruction in Contemporary Critical Theory.* Cambridge, Massachusetts: The MIT Press.
Mills, C. Wright. (1964). *Sociology and Pragmatism: The Higher Learning in America,* edited by Irving Louis Horowitz. New York: Paine-Whitman Publishers.
Mumford, Lewis. (1970). *The Myth of The Machine: The Pentagon of Power.* New York: Harcourt Brace Jovanovich, Inc.
Niebuhr, Reinhold. (1946). *Christianity and Power Politics.* New York: Charles Scribner's Sons.
_____. (1932/1960). *Moral Man and Immoral Society: A Study in Ethics and Politics.* New York: Charles Scribner's Sons.
Noddings, Nel. (1995). *Philosophy of Education.* Boulder, Colorado: Westview Press.
Novack, George. (1975). *Pragmatism Versus Marxism: An Appraisal of John Dewey's Philosophy.* New York: Pathfinder Press.
Ratner, Joseph. (1939). Introduction to John Dewey's Philosophy. *Intelligence In The Modern World: John Dewey's Philosophy,* edited by Joseph Ratner. New York: The Modern Library.
Reid, Thomas. (1803). *The Philosophical Works of Thomas Reid,* eighth edition, 2 volumes, edited and supplemented by Sir William Hamilton. Edinburgh, Scotland: James Thin.
Royce, Josiah. (1892/1930). *The Spirit of Modern Philosophy.* Cambridge, Massachusetts: The Riverside Press.
Ryan, Alan. (1995). *John Dewey and The High Tide of American Liberalism.* New York: W. W. Norton and Company.
Ryder, John. (1992). Community, Struggle, and Democracy: Marxism and Pragmatism. *John Dewey: Critical Assessments II,* edited by J. E. Tiles. New York: Routledge, 337-350.
Schneider, Herbert. (1946). *A History of American Philosophy.* New York: Columbia University Press.
Sleeper, Ralph. (1986). *The Necessity of Pragmatism: John Dewey's Conception of Philosophy.* New Haven, Connecticut: Yale University Press.
Spring, Joel. (1978). *American Education: An Introduction to Social and Political Aspects.* New York: Longman.
Spring, Joel. (1994). *Wheels In The Head: Educational Philosophies of Authority, Freedom, and Culture From Socrates To Paulo Freire.* New York: McGraw-Hill, Inc.
Tiles, J. E., editor. (1992). *John Dewey: Critical Assessments,* 4 volumes. London: Routledge.
Webb, Rodman B. (1976). *The Presence of The Past: John Dewey and Alfred Schutz on the Genesis and Organization of Experience.* Gainesville, Florida: The University Presses of Florida.
Weber, Max. (1905/1976). *The Protestant Ethic and the Spirit of Capitalism.* Translated by Talcott Parsons. New York: Charles Scribner's Sons.
West, Cornel. (1989). *The American Evasion of Philosophy: A Genealogy of Pragmatism.* Madison, Wisconsin: The University of Wisconsin Press.
_____. (1999). *The Cornell West Reader.* New York: Basic Books. White, Morton. (1943/1964). *The Origins of Dewey's Instrumentalism* (1943). New York: Octagon Books.

INDEX

FURTHER READING:

Deleuze, Education and Becoming

Inna Semetsky, *Monash University, Australia*

This wonderful, highly readable book breaks new ground in revealing commonalities between Deleuze's nomadic method of inquiry and the pragmatic method of John Dewey. It should be of great interest to both philosophers and educators.
NEL NODDINGS, *Stanford University,* author of *Happiness and Education.*

…few have placed the thinking of Dewey into effective dialogue with other forms of philosophy. Inna Semetsky's exciting new book bridges this gap for the first time by putting the brilliant poststructuralist work of Gilles Deleuze into critical and creative dialogue with that of Dewey. … The publication of this work announces the appearance of a remarkable line of thinking that scholars around the world will soon come to appreciate.
JIM GARRISON, *Virginia Polytechnic Institute and State University*, author of *Dewey and Eros.*

In this subtle and graceful study, Inna Semetsky brings together cultural and philosophical traditions long in need of connection… This is a significant and powerful work that is sure to invigorate discussions of educational theory for years to come.
RONALD BOGUE, *University of Georgia,* author of *Deleuze's Wake: Tribute and Tributaries.*

> Paperback ISBN: 90-8790-017-1
> Hardback ISBN: 90-8790-018-X
> November 2006, 156 pp
> SERIES: EDUCATIONAL FUTURES 3

Undead Theories
Constructivism, Eclecticism and Research in Education

David Geelan, *University of Queensland, Brisbane, Australia*

Theory is dead... long live theory! In this book David Geelan explores the contentious relationship between theory and research in education. The first chapter proclaims the 'death of theory' in educational research, but the remainder of the book explores a number of the ways in which theory survives and thrives. A commitment to conducting educational research that directly serves students and teachers, and that changes the life in classrooms through negotiation and collaboration, not through prescription, requires new tools and new ways of using them. Such tools include narrative modes of conducting and representing research as well as a 'disciplined eclecticism' that emphasises choosing and using competing theories in intentional ways. Metaphorical descriptions from the philosophy of science have been influential in science education. David explores the value of such perspectives, and argues that although they have offered important insights for science education, their use has also 'forced other perspectives into blindness'. In the contexts of research methodology, educational philosophy, science education and educational technology, David talks about new 'places to stand and ways to look' but, more importantly, gives specific examples of the ways in which these methodological tools and philosophical perspectives have been used in his own teaching and research practices.

Paperback ISBN:90-77874-31-3
Hardback ISBN:90-77874-32-1
April 2006, 160 pp

The Lost Dream of Equality
Critical Essays on Education and Social Class

John Freeman-Moir and Alan Scott, *University of Canterbury, New Zealand* **(eds.)**

This book examines the international hopes for equality in education over the past 60 years by looking at the current evidence and theory on social class and schooling. For more than half a century the relation between social class and education has been the subject of intense debate and political struggle, as well as the focus for the aspirations of millions of citizens and their children in Western democracies. This book will be relevant to teachers, advanced undergraduates and graduate students in the areas of the history, sociology and politics of education as well as policy analysis and applied social theory.

Paperback ISBN 90-8790-021-X
Hardback ISBN 90-8790-022-8
December 2006, 320 pp
SERIES: EDUCATIONAL FUTURES 5

For more information on these and other titles go to:
WWW.SENSEPUBLISHERS.COM

Printed in the United States
by Baker & Taylor Publisher Services